Laure
you are the
Keeper of the place
for your soul.
Wishing you continued
healing and much Love
and success!

Jan
Luther

Here's what others are saying about this book:

"Jan Luther's perspectives are insightful, unique, practical and comforting. This book should be required reading for everyone, both for dealing wisely with others who have had losses and for the tools we can use when ourselves are experiencing grief."

- **Mary Elizabeth Raines**, Author, *The Laughing Cherub Guide to Past-Life Regression: A Handbook for Real People* www.books-plays-scripts.com

"Nothing short of inspired."

- **Ann Adams**, LCSW www.FromtheDeskofAnnAdams.com

"There are many books about grief and grieving, but Jan Luther's stands alone as the only book that not only gives you a clear sense of how to come through the storms intact, but also shows you how to regain inner peace. Perhaps best of all, she introduces a remarkable mind-body tool into the process that works to physically and emotionally balance and restore your system to a place of serenity and health. I wish I had had this book when I went through the loss of my mother -if it had been available, I would have bought one for myself and one for everyone around me. Whether you have lost someone you love or you know someone who has, this book is essential -- you will be grateful, as I am, that Jan has written this. By putting the concepts and ideas here to work in your life, you will come through the grieving season stronger and more peaceful than you ever could have imagined."

- **Lynne Shaner**, MA, CHT, EFT Level 3 Practitioner and Trainer, Director of Praxis, www.eftpraxis.com, co-author of The EFTfree Manual and co-founder of www.EFTfree.net

"This is a powerful book. Jan does a great job of defining grief and giving direction on how to help yourself. I loved this book. It will be helpful to anyone experiencing loss, especially in those first couple of years."

- **Jerry Mudge**, Co-Founder, Footprints Ministry, Inc. For bereaved families in Charlotte, N.C.; Co-Founder, Our Children's Memorial Walkway in Charlotte, NC. www.angelfire.com/ny5/footprintsministry/

TRS PRESS

Charlotte, NC

ALSO BY JAN LUTHER

Mastering the Art of Success
*with New York Times Best Selling Author Jack
Canfield
(ISBN 978-1-60013-708-2)*

COMING SOON:

The 5 Aspects of Grief©

The EGO Tamer® Formulas for Success:
*How to Attract Fame, Fortune and Fabulous Sex;
if You Like Those Sorts of Things. (And Michael
wants beer!)*

Grief Is . . .
Mourning Sickness

"What to expect when you are grieving and what you can do about it!"

A Coaching Manual

Revised Edition

Jan Luther

Requests for permission should be addressed to:
The Rejuvenation Station, LLC
P.O. Box 624
Matthews, NC 28106
(704) 563-0874
Email: me@janluther.com

Grief Relief / Recovery, Success, Joy
Grief, Trauma, Loss & Change, Tapping
Recovery, Personal Peace
EFT® / Emotional Freedom Techniques®
Spirituality, Enlightenment

For more information:
www.JanLuther.com
www.GriefIsMourningSickness.com
www.TheEGOTamer.com

ISBN 978-0-9822454-1-5

Library of Congress Control Number: 2012936281

Design & Cover: Michael Luther
Photography: St. John's Photography
Manufactured in the United States of America

iv

Author's Note

When my 22-year old son died in a car accident, many lovely people gave me comforting gifts. The one that has had the most profound effect on me is a one-inch square quote card that says:

> *"I can be changed by what happens to me. But I refuse to be reduced by it."* - Maya Angelou

I still read that quote frequently. The message it carries has bolstered my resolve to remember that while I do not get to choose *what* I will experience in life, I always have the power to choose *how* I will respond to those experiences.

My primary goal in writing this book is to reduce your suffering. If you are willing to be open to new ideas about love, life and death, this book will help you save hours, months or even years of suffering and pain.

This book is based upon my own research and experience while successfully coaching thousands of clients through their tremendous life challenges of trauma, loss and change. I take full responsibility for my view points and my unique application of Tapping. Whenever I refer to a client case study in this book, I have used a fictitious name to protect their identity.

This revised edition has three primary changes from the first:
1. At the request of many readers I have included more of my own story.
2. After interviewing previous readers, I have infused the teaching points within actual client case studies to help them "stick."
3. I am including an overview of the **The 5 Aspects of Grief**© as a formula you can follow while using Tapping to heal your trauma, loss and grief.

Wishing you peace,

Jan

About the Author

Jan Luther, The EGO Tamer®, is one of nine U.S. **EFT Founding Master** practitioners, an AAMET Certified Trainer of Trainers, NLP Practitioner, Interfaith Minister and Life Skills Coach.

She is dedicated to taming the EGO - the little voice in the back of your head that wants to keep you focused on shame, disappointment and fear. By taming the EGO she liberates her audiences, students and clients so that they are free to experience courage, compassion and true connection and share their gifts and messages with the world. Through her innovative EGO Tamer formulas, she is able to take seemingly complicated life challenges and simplify them into **step-by-step strategies for success!**

Jan is available for speaking engagements, training workshops and weekend events. She also offers private personal sessions and topic-specific group workshops. Her workshops and events are not of the "cookie cutter" variety. Based on your input, Jan tailors her programs to the unique needs of your company or organization. Her signature topics include:

- **Maintaining Courage, Compassion and Connection During Times of Chaos and Change**

- **Healing the Five Aspects of Grief, a TLC3 Program:** Tools, Love and Coaching for Coping with the Tremendous Life Challenges of *Trauma, Loss and Change*
- **Building Your Indestructible Self-Worth**
- **Tearing Down Emotional Walls; Building Unconditional Love Relationships**
- **Plugging Into Your Financial Prosperity**

To book her at your next conference or event, please email her event coordinator at michael@janluther.com.

For speaking engagements, Jan travels from Charlotte, NC, where she lives with her husband, Michael, her three children and her five grandchildren.

Acknowledgements

When my editor read the first draft of this book, she commented that "God's fingerprints are all over this." I have to confess that I totally agree. I am humbled and grateful for the many earthly and heavenly angels that continue to support me in my work.

I want to thank my sweet husband, Michael. He is the love of my life and my greatest supporter. Anyone who knows us will tell you that we are connected at the heart; we are soul mates. He is the smartest and kindest man I know and I'm always amazed and so grateful that he is my husband and business partner. We have survived many life experiences together. Each experience has given us the opportunity to choose whether we will pull together or push away from each other. We continue to pull together. Not only do I know that I could not fulfill this "calling" without him, there is no doubt in my mind that his patience, love, and support were instrumental in my own survival and healing after losing our son.

And, of course, I want to thank my clients who are all amazing teachers. Every session allows me to teach what I need to learn.

And finally, I dedicate this book to those of you seeking to live your most authentic life.

x

Contents

Introduction

"It's so nice to meet you!"

I wish that we could sit together, you and me; face-to-face and knee-to-knee, maybe in my office or at your kitchen table.

If I could sit with you alone for just a little while, I know we would both be very blessed. I would then know better what you need. I could give you words of comfort. We all need comfort when our lives come crashing down around us. Or, if you needed courage, I would be your cheerleader igniting your faith and fanning the flames of your Soul.

The truth is that I am unable to discern what you need most from our time together through the pages of this book. So I pray, I envision, I beseech the Divine to direct my words in a way that will be meaningful to you and what you need - right now.

I do know that I didn't plan to be a grief coach. Even after the feeling of being called to serve was laid heavy on my heart, I have resisted. Like so many other "reluctant messengers" who find themselves at odds with calling themselves the expert, I have had to look long and hard at my life, my heart and my experiences before stepping out to offer a helping hand.

Grief doesn't seem like a very fun topic. I have a very playful childlike nature and grief seems like the opposite of that. But, God knows what He has ordained me to do and so, with humility, I extend to you my love, my empathy and my confidence that whatever your challenge has been, whatever trauma, loss or change has disrupted your life, I know without a doubt that you can recover and surpass the life you had expected and hoped for before. This is not the end of your story!

I am a professional griever. I didn't realize that about myself for a very, very long time. Now I playfully imagine myself at the "Grief Addicts Anonymous" meeting introducing myself:

"Hi, my name is Jan. I have been grieving since I was eight years old. I am trying to quit. I have read a lot of grief books. Some are really sad stories of how others have suffered through it. I know there are groups I could attend. I've tried some of them. Being the sensitive and empathetic girl that I am, I always left the meetings feeling more pain and sorrow than before I went in. I wish there was a manual about what to expect and what we can do about grief. Hey, maybe someday, I'll write one."

It is true, by the way. My first experience with trauma, loss and change (what I have discovered are the hallmarks of grief) was when I was in the second grade.

It was late summer when my parents brought me with them to visit a neighboring family who just happened to have a little girl about my age. We played and laughed and became instant friends. We were happily surprised when we discovered that fall that we were in the same class at school. We sat together, ate together and pretended to ride our ponies together during recess.

And then one day, my friend didn't come to school. I didn't think much of it, but what I did notice were the teachers. All morning long teachers from other classrooms would quietly slip into our classroom. They would stand next to our teacher at her desk with arms folded across their chests. Their faces were pale, their eyes red and puffy. The guest teachers would cock their head to one side as they whispered back and forth with our teacher. The short meetings would always end the same. The teachers would turn their backs to the class and there would be a short, but heavy silence. And then they would pat one another on the shoulder or rub the upper arm, nod and, as quietly as they came, the teachers would slip out of the classroom.

More than once, as they departed, I could feel them looking at me. Several times I caught them; their eyes were sad, apologetic almost. That day, and for many days after, our teacher talked a little more softly, looked at each of us with a little more tenderness and had more patience. Still, I couldn't help but sense that this all had something to do with me.

At recess after lunch, the whispering began on the playground; children whispering in one another's ears behind little hands. The child who was listening would become wide eyed and open mouthed; the teller of the secrets animated and serious. In the end, they would both look afraid.

Near the end of the day, I was beginning to wonder if I was in serious trouble. No one was whispering to me. In fact, I was certain that it was no longer my imagination; that I was, in fact, the only one they were not speaking to. I became painfully aware that everyone was...avoiding me.

Angry and hurt, I began to cry and was stomping my way toward the girl's bathroom when one of my girlfriends grabbed my hand and we ran into the bathroom together. She led me into a stall, closed and latched the door behind us, and like some sort of secret agent she proceeded to tell me a horrific story. With one hand on her hip and the other on my shoulder she matter-of-factly told me that my friend had been killed.

Now, this is pretty awful so if you are feeling emotionally raw, you might want to skip this next paragraph. But, I feel that if I am going to tell you the truth about who I am and how I got here, I need to tell you the whole truth as best I can.

It turned out that the reason my friend was not at school that day or ever after was that she and her sister had been drowned in the bathtub by her mother. And then her mother ran out into the freezing winter snow in her nightgown only to be found the next morning frozen to death in a field. The little girl told me that they had buried my friend in the ground by the church near the school.

I remember walking around the schoolyard as we were boarding the school bus, earnestly looking for my friend because I could not believe it was true. I didn't say anything to anyone about it, quite possibly for days.

I don't know how much time passed before I finally approached my mother and asked her to tell me if something had happened to my friend. I have a clear and vivid picture of my mother standing in front of the stove, stirring a large pot with a wooden spoon, tears streaming down her face, muffling sobs and speechless. Eventually she told me only the key points of the story. She explained that my friend's momma was very, very sad and that she was very sick.

After a few minutes I asked my mother if my friend was really buried by the school. I remember momma laughing and telling me that it was not true. I was relieved about that. Kids can really make up some crazy stories.

I know that experience changed me. We never spoke of it again and the kids at school dropped it soon, too. It was too gruesome to be enticing for long.

A few years after my girlfriend died, a young neighbor boy died of Leukemia. He was the brother of my new best friend. I know, I know - creepy, huh? But, that odd thought fortunately never occurred to me until I was in my thirties.

There were at least a half dozen near or fatal car accidents with young teens in our community over the next few years. Our family lost pets and several relatives. Soon my older siblings began moving out of the house. My oldest brother went to war in Vietnam. My oldest sister married a sailor and began traveling the world. One brother went on a church mission and another sister moved out to go to college. Being the sixth of seven children it was a little like losing my parents, siblings and my safety net all rolled into one! I was so sad, but didn't have the words or an outlet for it all.

Yes, I know you may be thinking, "Come on kid, these are just life experiences." Right? Well, one thing I am here to share with you is that these everyday experiences are filled to the brim with grief. It is the everyday experiences that can tear us up and wear us out over time. If we neglect to address them, they are the stealers of dreams and of our passion. Grief is truly an everyday experience. I used to believe that grief was solely designated to experiences when someone dies. Not so.

In fact, I invite you to take two minutes and think through your own life. Look for any memory of any experience that you wish you could have skipped in life. Write it down if you like. Seriously, stop reading for a minute and just ask yourself, "What are the pivotal and painful moments from my life?"

Have you ever been betrayed? Were you shocked, stunned or confused? Did you lose your sense of safety in the world for a time? Did something change? Did you find it hard to trust again? Yup, then you betcha, there is unresolved grief there!

7

Did you lose property to a flood, hurricane, tornado or a move? Uh...hello!! That is traumatic, right? And did you lose a sense of stability and community? Did things change after that? Uh-huh, more than you might have realized!

These life changing experiences...change us. Hopefully they help to refine us and make us stronger, more genuine and more compassionate people. I guess that is my goal as I write this coaching manual. I want to help you to somehow get it deep into your heart that stuff happens in life; how much of it sticks to you, well that's up to you.

So, what do I know about it?

I was born in Idaho in a town with less than 400 people. I never dreamed that my knight in shining armor would ride in on a Navy submarine, but he did. That first year of marriage felt like it would be the end of me.

We married in September. He was transferred to Bremerton, Washington in December (I remember driving through a snow storm when we moved!). His orders had him checking in by the first of January.

There I was, in what may well have been a foreign country. I didn't know another soul besides my husband and he, by the way, was suddenly working eighteen hours a day. We had one car which I was not much up to driving anyway. It didn't occur to me for months that I needed to find a job or a church. Being a very young wife, I was not even aware of the Navy Wives Club at the time.

Navy Life...

Fast forward nine years. During this time, we moved to – and from - four more cities. We now had four children and I was a volunteer leader in the Navy Wives Club. By this time I was getting into the groove of moving to a "new country" every 18 months or so.

I had learned how to manage the household; paying the bills, maintaining the house and yard and even changing the oil in our van. I was learning to be all things to the children, including resident counselor when they inevitably struggled with the stressors of military life. I was managing, but the stress and dis-ease was beginning to manifest physically.

At one point, I weighed over two-hundred and fifty pounds. I had regular migraines and suffered from chronic back pain. There was never a shortage of stress and grief with four children who, at that time, would have been between the ages of two and ten. And that was about the time that it happened; the death of one of our sailors.

There we were, 35 Navy wives sullen and scared sitting at the Navy Family Service Center. A young woman stood in front of us with her polyester skirt and matching blazer. Her light colored silk blouse was tied in a big floppy bow at the neckline. Her shoes had high heels and her nails had polish. She was not "one of us."

We were the Navy wives; we wore blue jeans and t-shirts, tennis shoes and pony tails. We mostly had unpolished and short finger nails. I knew every one of these ladies. We were a sisterhood. I knew which wives had children, which ones had paying jobs, which ones were naughty and which ones were nice.

We often half-joked that as Navy Wives we were not "issued with our husband's sea bags" so we perceived ourselves as something of a necessary evil that the powers that be had to deal with from time to time. This was one of those times. We had been strongly encouraged to attend this meeting with the Navy appointed grief counselor.

It was the cruelest of ironies. The submarine had returned from an uneventful three month deployment. Everybody was so happy to be reunited. Sometime within weeks of their return, several of the guys decided to hit the gym and play a pickup game of basketball. In the middle of the game our friend and fellow sailor, Danny, fell to the floor of the gym. We learned that he had died of a heart attack.

I was in my late twenties and as I sat in that room with my Navy wife peers, I realized I was one of the older wives. Usually, I took on that role with passion and big-sisterly purpose. On that particular day, we were all equally frightened little girls with our heads full of fearful questions.

"What really happened?"

"Will Wendy – his wife - get to stay in base housing for a while?"

"What about her finances? Will she get benefits? Will the Navy pay for her to move home? Will they help her get a job?"

"What will become of her precious little toddler?"

And the question no one would ever ask: "What would I do if I were Wendy?"

Wendy was not even thirty years old and now she was a widow. That was a terrifying thought for all of us.

The poised young counselor answered our timidly asked questions as best she could. Once she felt she had allayed the most pressing fears, she switched modes and began her presentation.

She had a couple of poster boards and some pamphlets and she droned on about the five stages of grief. She implored us to be sure and let our Ombudsman or the family clinic doctor know if our husbands began to exhibit any of a list of warning signs of depression.

And then she handed out more papers and we politely obliged her in passing them hand-to-hand from one woman to another around the room. I watched as the stack of papers got closer and closer and smaller and smaller. I secured my copy and began to read ahead to drown out the instructor's too calm voice. It didn't match the frenetic energy in the room. I needed to focus on something else.

On the paper there were about two dozen questions. They started out simple enough:

"Over the past four weeks, how often would you say that you have felt stressed?" The multiple choice answers were given in a range of "Never" to "Daily".

"How often do you feel tired?"

"Do you feel depressed?"

I skimmed quickly over the questions and then my eyes hit a speed bump and I came to a screeching halt:

"Do you ever think about suicide?"

I immediately bristled as I thought to myself, "No, I am not thinking of suicide! Do they really think I am going to answer these questions? Are they planning to collect these forms at the end of the meeting? This is some serious stuff they are asking about!"

We each finished our little self-evaluations and *then* the counselor thought to inform us that no one would see our answers and we could keep the papers and take them home.

Then she began talking about stress and grief. Now, I don't know if you have ever gotten the giggles in a totally inappropriate situation, but it happened to me on that occasion. This was one of those times that the sheer absurdity of this woman talking to us about stress under the current circumstances just tickled my funny bone. I was able to keep myself quiet, but I was shaking my head to myself incredulously as we then reviewed the list of the top "life stressors."

We were all clearly stressed to a supreme and overloaded degree. We were all struggling with the crazy mix of emotions of grief and terror for Wendy and the guilt and shame of being grateful that it was not happening to us!

You see, while none of the wives ever talked about it, every time that submarine floated out of the Puget Sound, every wife said a little prayer that we would not be sitting exactly where Wendy was this day.

So, imagine my chagrin when I read the top three stressors according to the list:
- Death of a loved one
- Divorce
- Moving

"Are you KIDDING ME?" I thought to myself. "That is military life every stinkin' day!"

Every time a military family moves, they leave behind their entire community support system: church, neighbors, friends and often family. It is akin to burying everyone you love at one time. Now don't get ahead of me. I know - now more than ever - that military families have resources to stay in touch while on deployment. However, submariners get an allotment of what is called a "family gram" – a one-way message from their wife. Let me see if I can put it into perspective for you. Imagine tweeting to your spouse in fifty words or less only five or six times over a three-month period. They cannot tweet back. It is like the carefully crafted message goes out into the ethers and you never know if or who will read it. True story!

So, have you ever moved? How many weeks did it take before you unpacked the last boxes? How many months before you began to feel like you knew your way around the town and were getting to know your neighbors? For many military families - at least back in the day when I was in the rank and file among them - we designated certain boxes that were not to be unpacked at each house simply because we knew we would not need the items enough to devote space to them. So, as you know, moving is stressful and some military families do it almost yearly; often without the help of their deployed service member.

So now we come to the divorce stress. Military families have a high divorce rate. The civilian divorce rate is nothing to celebrate either. What folks may not be aware of is that every time our spouses left on deployment, we were essentially "separating" and we dealt with many of the same emotional states as a couple divorcing.

One unique phenomenon is what I used to call preparatory grief. Whenever our men would deploy we would steel ourselves for the unknown and the unimaginable. It is a sense of being prepared for the worst (war or death of our spouses) so that we can feel prepared to manage the dreaded thought of losing our loved one. Being ever vigilant in that manner takes a tremendous toll on the soul.

When the deployment is over and the reintegration period occurs, there is both excitement and tremendous fear. Time, distance and life stresses change people. There is an unspoken fear of, "Who will this person be when they return?"

One of my husband's duty stations was a ballistic missile submarine which had a three-month cycle wherein he was either 'in port' at home working at the training and refit facilities or 'out to sea' on the submarine where they were virtually dead and gone to us for three months. There were two crews on each ship. One crew was out to sea while the second crew was home.

The emotional cycle would begin as soon as the alternate crew returned home from sea. The honeymoon was over and the men's schedule would go from a lovely 7:00 AM to 4:00 PM work day to 12-hour days with every third day being a 24-hour duty day. This eventually transitioned into shiftwork – seven days a week of 12 hours on and 12 hours off. They were in what is called refit, meaning they perform a mini-overhaul of the entire submarine to ensure it was sea worthy for their next three-month deployment.

For the first several weeks, the main stressor of shiftwork is getting the family to function around when daddy is sleeping.

Then, it starts to sink in that daddy is getting ready to leave again. As a good mommy, I would begin initiating conversations with the children to help them be prepared for daddy leaving.

Sure enough, after a few weeks of this rigorous work schedule daddy would be coming home more and more exhausted. He would do the military version of stop, drop and roll: stop for a little kiss, drop his clothes all in the corner of the room and then roll into the bed with the gentle reminder that "Daddy needs some sleep, so please keep the kids quiet!"

About this time mommy would start getting a little pissy. All of the little voices in the back of her head (what I call the fear-based or EGO voices) would start whining. "He doesn't have any time for us. It is not fair that I have to do everything around here...I didn't sign up for all of this!" I think you get the idea. Poor, poor, pitiful me!

And as you might have guessed, we would start fighting over... well, everything. That would lead to cold shoulders, avoidance, and, unfortunately, harsh words. Then one day, daddy would get up at the crack of dawn, walk out the front door and disappear for three months.

It would take about two weeks before the sadness kicked over into regret. I would feel so guilty at having been so selfish, impatient and unloving. Then I would start with the bargaining prayers: "God, I am so sorry I was not supportive. Please bring him home safely."

There were many nights I would put the children to bed and clean house late into the night out of sheer distress. And then...about six weeks into the deployment; acceptance - or at least resignation to our new normal - would once again emerge. The children and I would get into a routine. I would begin writing the love notes that I would stuff into a shoe box and send out to sea with my husband on his next deployment a few months away.

So as I sat in this meeting that dreary morning in the Navy Family Service Center, I felt as if I had just awakened to a great secret: <u>we were living in a constant state of grief</u>. There were constant traumas, losses and the persistent companion: CHANGE. I vowed that day that I would learn about these grief stages. I made a heart-centered decision that I would somehow learn to anticipate and paddle with the ever-changing tides of grief.

With this information I began initiating conversations with my husband. We came to agreements about what we needed at each stage and we gave each other permission to work through the anger, fear and sadness without taking it out on each other. We came up with our own sort of "code words" that signaled what we were feeling so that we were quickly able to stop taking it all so personally. I am honored to share with you that not only were we able to manage the transitions with greater ease, but those years of practice at successfully navigating grief laid the foundation for my path of understanding that we are never really at the mercy of our emotions.

That is my primary purpose for writing this book. I want to help. I want to show you the map I have drawn through my lifetime tours of grief. I want to share some possible shortcuts - and point out a few of the danger zones - as you travel through the valley of grief. Hopefully, through the stories and examples I share, you will be entertained, inspired and educated.

You may be living in Canada or half way around the world for all I know, but through this amazing medium of the written word, you and I can work through this together. Our paths may cross one day; maybe not. For today, I want to offer you words of encouragement. Information that I think - I deeply hope - will help reduce your suffering and inspire you to live your Divine Purpose sooner, happier, and better in some little way.

So, now for the part I have resisted long enough...sharing my story. The "and then one day" that changed everything.

August 5, 2006...

The phone awakened me from a sound sleep. I rolled over to see the neon red digital clock face reading 3:33 am. "It's probably another wrong number." I grumbled to myself.

I cleared my throat and reached for the receiver.

"Hello." The rasp in my sleepy voice should have made it obvious that whoever was calling had awakened me from a deep sleep.

The deep male voice was calm and unapologetic as he cut right to the chase, "Hello, who am I speaking with?"

At least he's speaking English, I thought to myself as I flashed back to previous late night calls from Spanish and Chinese speaking callers.

"This is Mrs. Luther." I said impatiently.

"Mrs. Luther, do you know Devin Luther?"

My breath caught in my throat. My mind and body snapped to attention and I sat straight up in the bed.

"Yes," I paused, "I am Devin's mother."

"Mrs. Luther, this is State Patrolman Fischer. There has been an accident involving Devin's car and we are not sure who was driving. We need you to come to the hospital."

There was a symphony of voices in my head. "What does he mean they don't know who was driving? What if it was my other son David? Was it his friend Brandon? Where was the accident? How did he get my number? Is he okay?" So many internal questions; I was feeling increasingly panicked by the second.

I took a breath and asked the man, "How bad is it?"

"Pretty bad."

In order to calm all the noise in my head I started coaching myself: "Do not write a story, we do not know anything. Do not write a story, there is nothing I can do from here. Get up. Go to the hospital. One step at a time."

My husband, Michael, was awake now.

I quickly relayed the two tidbits of information that I was given. "There's been an accident involving Devin's car. We need to go to the hospital."

There is silence.

I force myself to stay calm. I brush my teeth. I take a 2-minute shower while Michael dresses. Every move I make feels like it is time-warped. I put on my jeans and a t-shirt. I quickly decide that I will have to wear my glasses because my contact solution didn't have time to neutralize the peroxide solution.

I thought, "Shall we wake our daughter Jami?" My mind immediately answered, "No, not until we know what is going on."

We step out into the garage and the hot August air hits my lungs and makes me gasp.

As the garage door opens, it reveals the pitch dark of the early dawn hour. The little pickup truck engine chatters to a start.

Out of the garage. Onto the highway. We don't say a word.

It feels like we are moving in slow motion. All the other cars seem to be passing us. As always, Michael is abiding by the speed limit and he is doing a great job of making it look like he is focused on his driving.

I am torn between the urge of wanting to tell him to please hurry and the even bigger urge to stop everything. I am so afraid.

I was afraid to look him in the eyes. What would I do if he looked as frightened as I was? So, we just rode along in the dark.

Without being prompted we both looked at the dashboard clock and then quickly glanced at each other after watching the numbers click over to 4:13.

We both straightened up and looked front. Suddenly, I heard him groan, "Oh, God." He faintly whispered. I had to look at him now.

His face went white. I tried to control the feeling of panic. "What? What do you know?" I was trying to guard my tone but it was impossible to hide my agitation.

He seemed to be sucking in air. He could hardly speak, but said, "I just saw his car on the back of a tow truck. It's bad."

Those words, "It's bad" hit me in the stomach. All the air went out of me. I know my husband doesn't exaggerate. He does not like drama. If he said it's bad, I might have described it as horrendous.

I couldn't ask. I didn't want to know if it (the car) was totaled or torn apart or if the front end was sitting in the trunk.

My father was a small town mechanic and I had seen more than my share of "death mobiles" growing up. I gave myself a new set of instructions: Just breathe. Don't let your mind imagine what that car looked like. It doesn't matter.

Then, I was all in. All of my inner resistance about making this trip flew out the window. I didn't say a word, but every cell in my body decided: GET ME TO THE HOSPITAL!

Every red light seemed to mock our sense of urgency. The fear was affecting my stomach. I drew on my knowledge of EFT and started tapping quietly. "I will not be sick. I will not throw up..."

Finally, we exited the highway and pulled into the hospital parking lot. I am immediately grateful that he was driving. I realize now that I didn't have the clarity of mind to even know where to go.

We park in the nearly deserted lot at the emergency room.

Michael takes my hand. I feel really odd. I can see him holding my hand, but I don't feel it.

Tap, tap, tap..."be here... be right here in this body...present now."

We swiftly walked up to the hospital. As the sliding glass doors swooshed open, the first person I see is a male nurse standing behind the glass window under the bright red "Check-In" sign. He looks...very, very, sad.

Then I see two state patrolmen. I don't see their faces. Instead, my eyes choose to focus in on the top of patrolman's hat.

"Hmm...Tassels," I thought. "I didn't know that their hats had tassels."

The two men approach us. My little EGO voice goes off in my head, "What do they want? They don't know us!"

One of the troopers steps forward, "Mr. and Mrs. Luther?"

I can't look at his face. Michael answered, "Yes."

"I am so sorry"....he continued apologetically and took a breath... "Your son didn't make it."

Then, he shoved a little blue zipper pouch into my hand. It looked like a cosmetic case. I didn't understand. This isn't mine, why is he giving me this?

My ears feel hot.

"I don't want this" I think to myself.

Then, on the third ragged breath, the realization hits me. This little pouch that fits in the palm of one hand contains all that is left of my son's personal belongings. I see his wallet. I see his car keys. I tilt and turn the pouch around with my thumbs.

The hot stinging tears begin to stream down my cheeks.

There is a high pitched screeching sound in my ears. I feel dizzy, I am filled with rage. I bite my lip just so that I can keep my tongue quiet.

Did I forget how to breathe? I am gasping in tiny little gulps of air like a fish out of water.

I am struck that one part of my mind seems so calm and strong and there is another part of my mind is screeching in my head, "No, no... I don't think so. You have made a mistake."

I can see that my hands are shaking so I force myself to clutch the little blue pouch. "Don't drop it. Don't throw it. Don't have a fit. Not here. Not now. Stay calm."

All of this has taken place in both a slow-motion eternity and a nanosecond.

That was the day that everything changed.

The patrolman interrupted my inner dialogue by saying, "We need someone to identify the body."

Michael tells them he will go.

I hear my voice angry, insistent, "NO, NO, I want to go, I need to see him!"

I immediately thought, "Really? We are going to the morgue?" Part of my mind is hyper-alert and very present. The other part of my mind that I think of as the "little voice" or the EGO mind has gone insane. I hear it yelling and cursing at the men, "What the hell is going on? This cannot f***ing be right. You will see, we will get down there and it will be some other poor mother's son!"

The male nurse has taken the lead now and says, "Will you follow me, please?"

We take our little sad parade down the hallway. Everyone seems to be clearing a path for us. Into an elevator we go. My nervous hands are sweating and I am clutching the little blue pouch like it is my ticket out of here.

The elevator doors open as we reach the lowest level of the hospital. The hallway is so dark. The dimly lit walls are illuminated by the occasional security light. Michael and I are following the male nurse. The two patrolmen are in tow behind us.

Like dazed people walking through a maze, we blindly follow the nurse to who knows where. The silence has an echo. No one is saying a word. What is there to say?

Each breath I take seems tighter and shallower. My years of meditation training kicked in and I began to focus on the air moving through my nose and into my lungs. In through my nose...fill up lungs...damn it, why don't my lungs work?

And we keep walking; walking through the vacant dark hallways.

How long is this hallway? I can hear my flip-flops. They are so loud in the silence. My legs are threatening to buckle. Suddenly, I have one obsessive thought. My mind is as quiet as a night in the desert against the sound of the pop-pop-popping of my flip flops. Oh, God! Can't I walk quieter? I mumble something like, "Are we there yet?"

No one answers.

Finally, we come to the end of the hallway. There appears to be a small room to one side. It looks more like a closet than a room. No windows just light wood paneling. The hallway forks and divides into two diverging hallways around the little room.

The male nurse (did he ever introduce himself?) holds his palm out at us in the stop position and says, "I just need a minute."

I look behind him and there is a small sign on the door - MORGUE.

"OH, GOD!" I whimpered. My stomach drops to my knees. Michael puts one hand on my shoulder and says "I'll do it."

29

Without hesitating, I command, "No, I want to!"

After a few seconds the male nurse steps out of the room and into the hallway toward us. He says, "He's ready" as he backs toward the room as if to beckon us toward him.

The door opens. The room is so small; too small. How can this be a morgue? There are four or five metal tables riveted onto the center wall stacked one over the other like a baker's rack. Several of the racks contain black zippered bags. One tray is pulled out away from the wall and is tilting at a slight angle. The black bag is zipped open about 25 inches.

There, on the table, peaking out of the black bag, just above the zipper, is the face of our son; my baby boy. It is Devin.

I hear Michael gasp, "Oh, Buddy."

We stand like statues looking at him. He is wearing the blue pinstripe shirt that I bought him for Christmas.

His eyes are partially open. I can see just a sliver of his hazel brown eyes. Those eyes that always looked like they were filled with mischief are cold and empty now. They look like glass. The spark that everyone knew to be Devin was gone.

There are cuts on his face. His blonde hair is wet and matted.

I reach out and touch his head and quickly draw my hand back. He, that body, it used to be my boy. But, the light is gone. His hair feels stiff. The body looks and feels like wax.

Then, I feel a tremendous pressure on my chest. Being highly empathic, I have always sensed what others are feeling, but this was a first for me. This was an after-the-fact sensation. They had not told us anything about the accident. I had no idea what had actually happened, but in that moment I felt a crushing blow to my chest. I immediately discerned that this was his experience. I was picking up on what he felt at the accident.

My voice is shrill as I blurt out, "OH GOD- HE HIT SOO HARD!!!"

"OH, oh, buddy..."

It feels like all of the air has been sucked out of the room. I am softly weeping now. The nurse steps up with a box of tissues and, in a fit, I push them away and bury my head in Michael's shoulder.

I can't feel him holding me. I want to say, "Tighter, hold me, tighter. I feel like I am going to explode into a million pieces and fly apart all over this room." But, I cannot speak.

I am quivering. My knees feel like jelly. I am using sheer will to stay standing upright.

Michael is just staring at the form on the metal slab. It is as if he is frozen in-between worlds. He is softly crying. I can see the pain and anguish in his face.

I look to see the three men standing to our left. I reach out and the male nurse intuitively holds out the tissue box.

How long did we stand there? What were they thinking? I don't remember hearing a single sound, but my eyes captured a dozen pictures and burned them into my brain.

Pity. That is what I saw on their faces. I knew we had to go back down the hall and into the elevator again, but I don't remember walking back to the elevator or reaching the main floor of the hospital. I didn't hear my flip flops. It was like I had left my body and gone out of the building. I was out of my body somewhere, nowhere. Not at the hospital. I just don't remember.

The next thing I do remember is the male nurse telling us that he needs us "to decide." Decide? Decide what? I wondered what he could possibly mean and then the bits and pieces of his sentences started to make sense. He wanted to know if we wanted to donate Devin's organs. Devin had it on his driver's license that he wanted to donate his organs.

Michael looked at me and flinched. I could feel his questioning hesitation. "Yes, yes of course," I said.

The nurse then led us into a storage closet; literally, a storage room. Chairs are stacked in two corners and there are two or three open chairs to sit on. There is one small table with a phone on it. The nurse picks up the phone and punches some buttons.

I can't quite make sense of what he is saying, but there is a sense of urgency and impatience in his voice. He hands the phone to Michael.

I can't sit or I think I will melt into a puddle. So I stand up and I begin to pace the three steps back and forth. It is dizzying, so I stop and just sway from side-to-side. I folded my arms tight around my torso. I hear Michael talking, but his voice doesn't sound right.

He seems annoyed at the questions; annoyed that he has to do this now; annoyed that he is supposed to know the right answers at a time like this.

He is barking out the answers to the mysterious voice on the other end of the phone, "Yes, No, No, No, NO, NO, NO!"

I am feeling like a caged animal. I wanted to run out of that room, run out of that hospital, run back to bed and wake up from this nightmare.

My little voice is ranting inside my head again, "How long will this take? How many questions? Is Michael okay?"

I couldn't get sense of his energy. My own energy was totally scrambled. Can we go now? Are we done yet? Let me out of here!

Again, I notice the male nurse. This time I am very aware that he is staring at me. I cannot imagine what he is thinking. His expression is unclear to me. Is he confused? Is he curious? Is he annoyed that I am pacing like a panther in a cage?

I decide that I really don't give a flip what he thinks.

After what seemed like an eternity, Michael hands the phone back to the nurse and he stands up and quickly ushers me out of that closet.

Finally done with all the ridiculous questions, we are charging out of the hospital. What had been a vacant parking lot and lobby when we arrived is now filled with cars and people. There are people everywhere. People seem to be milling around and coming from every direction. We marched with determination through the people and out the glass doors into the sunlight. I've lost all sense of time. I just want to get away. Away, to a place where I can breathe. Away so I can cry. I want to look at Michael and see him looking confidently at me that we are going to be okay.

Michael leads me straight to the pickup and around to my side door. I couldn't hold it in any longer. I threw my arms around his neck and I sobbed; great long sobs, sucking in air, my chest heaving and quaking as I wept. Finally, catching my breath, my legs gave out and he gently hoisted me onto my seat.

I don't remember leaving the parking lot. I think I asked if he was okay to drive. I know I certainly was not. How did he do that?

And then, we were home.

I couldn't quit pacing. I needed something to do to feel normal. I went to my bedroom and dumped out my sock drawer.

Michael came into the room. "I know." I said, apologetically. "This is weird, but I have to do something with my hands or I will lose my mind."

"It's okay, baby. You do whatever you need to do, okay?"

In that moment, I could not comprehend the huge mix of emotions. His complete acceptance and understanding, no pressure, no judgment, just the man I loved giving me perfect permission to feel and respond however I needed to was truly the beginning of my healing.

He began to make phone calls. I don't know how. I couldn't even think. "HOW can he make calls?" I thought.

I finished rearranging my sock drawer and paced around and around until I couldn't be in the house any more.

He asked if we should wake Jami and tell her. It wasn't even 8:00 AM yet, so I said, "No. Let her sleep. It's going to be a very long day."

Out of the house and into the yard, I found myself marching toward our tree stump. Two months previous to his death, Devin and I had devoted an entire weekend to chopping up and stacking the limbs of the pear tree that had fallen during a storm. This was the last place we had spent time together.

I was craving something, anything that would connect me to him. Sitting on the stump, I wept quietly as my mind jumped from memory to memory, trying to find something, anything that would make me feel Devin again.

Sitting there on the stump I battled with the little EGO voices in my head.

"What am I supposed to do now?"
"How can I tell the children?"
"How can I live with this pain?"

In a moment of despair I cried out to God, "Help me!" and I heard the familiar whisper of spirit say, "You are the same person that you were yesterday. You will get through this."
We told the children.

People came. There were family members and lovely neighbors who brought food. There were flowers and cards and money to help with the expenses.

My sisters flew in from Idaho.

We chose the burial plot, the head stone and the casket.

We had the funeral.

In the days that followed, we drove out to see where the accident was. We stopped by his trailer to see what we would have to do to take care of his belongings.

We stopped at the junk yard where they had towed his car so we could see it.

We emptied his trailer.

That entire week was a blur.

We had so many visitors and phone calls. Neighbors we had never met brought in food to ease some of the burden.

One of those first mornings, my friend Kelly came to support me. She was so gentle and yet so strong. She asked me to describe how I was feeling and I had to really focus on what I was feeling to try and give her a metaphor. I told her it was like labor but in reverse. When we deliver a baby, our body begins the birthing pain slowly; slowly and steadily the pain amplifies until we reach a breaking point where we think we will die before we birth the child. I was feeling like I was going to die. It was as if I had suddenly been thrown into the bearing down and pushing stage of labor. Everything hurt; my belly was filled with feelings of terror. In that moment I could not imagine living through this.

But, I did. And before I knew it, a week had passed. On Saturday morning my sisters repacked their bags and we were off to see a little bit of the city before we had to take them to the airport.

There was a steady, heavy rain that morning, but my sisters asked if we could stop by the cemetery first.

The fresh mound of dirt was symbolic of our fresh grief. The rain had made little puddles of mud around the edges. Four potted flowers that had been placed around the site had been undisturbed, but were losing their bloom.

It was quiet.

The memory and emotion of the burial service only three days before skidded across my mind and lay heavy on my heart.

We all huddled under our umbrellas, arms around waists and shoulders. I will be eternally grateful that they were all there with me for that first of many visits to his graveside.

After a short drive around some of our lovely Charlotte neighborhoods, we drove to the airport. Standing under the "departing" sign felt poignant to me as we hugged and said our good-byes.

Michael and I drove home. There wasn't much to say. We were both weary with grief.

I had purposely kept one client phone appointment for that afternoon. It seemed to me that some sense of normalcy needed to be established quickly.

The session was profoundly helpful for the client. Ironically, he was processing trauma from his childhood, some twenty years earlier; watching his little brother get hit by an automobile. Being able to step into my role as comforter and coach and have a successful session was huge for me.

When everything feels so different, it's easy to imagine you will never be the same. Familiar things like brushing your teeth, cleaning out a sock drawer and doing your job seem different. But, it's these little - and often mundane - things in life that feel manageable when your life feels out of control.

There was little, if any, sleeping that night or any night for many to come. On Monday morning I got out a spiral notebook and wrote on the front of it:

Grief is . . . Mourning Sickness

Jan Luther

Grief Is . . . Mourning Sickness

The process of "birthing" or bringing a life into this world is mirrored in reverse by the process of "deathing" or releasing a life from this world.

When our youngest daughter, Jami, first discovered she was pregnant, she was ecstatic. She has wanted to have a baby for years. She immediately made an appointment with her OB/GYN.

As Jami was well aware, women experience changes in their body in support of carrying the fetus. Some women experience daily bouts of what is referred to as "morning sickness." The flu-like symptoms of morning sickness are different for each woman and are quite unpredictable. Ironically, "morning" sickness symptoms may manifest themselves at _any_ time of the day or night.

Fortunately, Jami didn't have any morning sickness.

Over the next nine months, there was a constant focus on her health and wellness and on the preparation for bringing a new life into the world. Her doctors constantly stressed the importance of getting plenty of rest, watching her diet, and getting fresh air and exercise.

She stopped drinking alcohol and caffeine. She's never been a smoker, so that was easy. She was conscientious about taking her prenatal vitamins and, when it became necessary, added iron pills.

Jami has always loved children. One of her favorite jobs was as an Activity Director at a local country club where she provided childcare and activities for the members' children. Additionally, she helped care for her two nephews and twin nieces from the time they were newborns. So, in other words, she was more experienced with children than most young women her age.

During her monthly visits to her OB/GYN they would monitor the growth and health of both the fetus and the mother. She purchased several books and did countless hours of research on the internet regarding birth, delivery and child rearing.

Her days begin to fill up with thinking, planning and doing the innumerable tasks that must be accomplished before the baby arrives. As it so often happens in life, once our family's attention was on our expectant mother, it seemed we saw more expectant mothers everywhere.

As her belly grew, complete strangers would approach her and ask about her progress.

"When are you due?"

"Is this your first?"

"Can I touch your belly?"

Everyone seemed to have a story or some advice about their own pregnancies, their own children or their grandchildren.

As the due date approached, our family and friends began to rally around her. There were baby showers and well wishes and offers to assist with whatever she needed.

During the last month there were weekly birthing classes and not just one, but two tours of the hospital birth and delivery floor.

I have never seen a mother more prepared for labor and delivery than Jami. She had a marvelous pregnancy. She worked up until one week before her due date.

Her labor began at 2:00 AM on September 10th. She knew she could expect to be in labor for up to 36 hours before the baby was born so she had outlined several plans for keeping herself busy during the early stages of labor.

Part of her plans included a special lunch out with me. During our lunch together, her contractions were slow and steady and about eight minutes apart. Then we went shopping at a local craft store. She was very calm. When a contraction would come on, she would simply stop walking and breathe. After an hour or so at the craft store, we moved on to a local clothing store.

At this point, she had been in labor for nearly 12 hours. The contractions were happening about six minutes apart and were getting much stronger. She was having more and more difficulty walking around. It was time to go home.

In her research, Jami found an amazing iPhone app for tracking the contractions. This was just one of the many cool things she introduced me to throughout her pregnancy. Mothers are much more educated and involved in their birth and delivery than I was when my last child was born some 23 years earlier.

Back home, we did final checks on her hospital bag and she tried to rest. She would alternate between resting and walking around the neighborhood until her contractions were about five minutes apart.

She continued this until around 10:30 PM when the contractions started getting much stronger and it was getting nearly impossible for her to remain calm. It was time to go to the hospital.

The car ride was miserable. She simply could not get comfortable. After the 15-minute ride, we were checking her in at the labor and delivery unit just as we had rehearsed.

When the doctor examined her, she was dilated only two centimeters. She was so discouraged. After 18 hours of labor she was just certain that she would be closer to delivering the baby. The doctor honored her wishes to not be on an IV or to be attached to the birthing monitors. She was allowed to walk, to use the birthing ball, to rock in the rocking chair; whatever would make her process the most comfortable for her.

The labor became more and more taxing. Each contraction was lasting longer and the breaks between contractions were getting shorter. At 3:00 AM on September 11th, she was dilated to three centimeters. I could see that Jami was beginning to despair.

The next check was at 5:50 AM and she was only at four centimeters. I wasn't sure if she was just exhausted or if she was feeling desperate that it was taking so long, but as soon as the doctor left the room her countenance changed.

She would not be comforted and was now asking for an epidural. I tried to coach her, reminding her of the many reasons she had wanted to deliver naturally. Her nurse suggested more movement, walking or sitting on the birthing ball. She was not interested. She wanted medication! We decided to call the doctor and initiate the procedure for an epidural.

Thanks to her wonderful birthing instructor, Jami fully understood that she would have to go on an IV, be on constant monitoring, and not be able to move around. She also knew she would have to take in one bag of IV fluid before they could give her the epidural. By that point she was, as they say, "over it" and wanted the IV. She was prepared to suffer the next 20-30 minutes in order to get the pain relief of the epidural.

She was in excruciating pain. She could not get comfortable. She was having the urge to push and was panicky because she knew that at four centimeters, it wasn't time to push.

When the doctor came in at 6:15 AM to examine her and give the order for her epidural, he was shocked. The baby's head was crowning. He called for baby meds and someone from pediatrics. Jami was frightened. Was something wrong? "No," Dr. Moore said. "You are about to have this baby, so there's no time for an epidural."

The pain had taken over and Jami was not her usual self. She was in serious pain. She just wanted me to leave her alone! I could no longer get her to focus and breathe with me, so in my very best Mom voice I sternly told her, "Jami, the only way to it...is through it! Get yourself together and talk yourself through this!"

Dr. Moore told her to push with her next contraction.

She pushed hard, but I could see she was still panicking. Then she started talking to herself... "Come on Jami, you got this!" Two contractions and four pushes later, baby McKenna was born at 6:47 AM on September 11, 2011.

They immediately put the baby on her chest and all the pain was gone. Everyone was teary and celebrating. Dr. Moore even patted her on the back saying, "That was a really good job." Everyone was astounded that in less than one hour, this first-time Momma had gone from being dilated only four centimeters to holding her baby. Once she made up her mind to focus and follow the doctor's instructions, she found her strength and made quick work of delivering the baby.

Being with my lovely daughter through this extra special experience reminded me that my assessment over the years was right on.

Birthing a child and "deathing" a child are very similar.

From the moment I got the news that my son had died, the physical and emotional pain was excruciating. In fact, I can now see that, in many ways, the physical process of grieving is the exact reverse of delivering a child. It was as if I had entered the final, transitional stage of labor first.

There was sudden and incessant nausea and shock. I was inconsolable and my inner voices were screaming, "No, I don't want to do this! This cannot be happening. Make it stop!"

It took great concentration for me to breathe. My entire body hurt. I felt like an elephant was sitting on my chest and that my lungs had collapsed. I was physically weak to the core.

I had to will myself not to throw up, to stand upright. Every step from the entrance of the hospital to the morgue took my complete focus.

Once we left the hospital, my head was spinning. The car ride was miserable. I wanted to jump out. I wanted to just go to sleep. I really didn't know what I wanted. I just know I was in excruciating pain; inconsolable.

Once we returned home from the hospital, my amazing husband was able to make a few phone calls.

Within the hour, one of his friends came to see him and then, soon after, his father came to offer comfort and support. I was not ready to talk to anyone. I just wanted to be left alone.

By that afternoon, his family had all gathered at our home. Before I knew it, a group of neighbors from his sisters' neighborhood had brought in food, drinks, and paper supplies to help us care for the approaching throng of guests.

It took me several hours to find my voice and finally call my sisters. They immediately began making arrangements for the trip to North Carolina from Idaho.

I was experiencing full blown "<u>mourning</u> sickness."

It was the beginning of many months where I had no appetite. I was not able to sleep. Every waking moment those first few days was consumed with thinking and planning and doing the innumerable tasks that needed to be accomplished in preparation for the funeral. It was clear that my mind had been hijacked by obsessive thoughts of Devin, his life, his death and my fear that I could not live through all of this pain.

For months on end, I read books, listened on line and attended live grief support meetings. Often, I would feel worse afterward. Nothing seemed to be what I was looking for. Out of sheer necessity, I began earnestly studying scripts and notes from sessions and workshops I had led with my clients on releasing trauma and dealing with grief.

As I pored over the files and listened to the recordings, I made notes of the things that rang most true and helpful to me as I walked my path of recovery. I was looking for any predictable patterns, for some of the best suggestions, advice and new perceptions that would help me quickly get my life back. All the while, as I coached myself, I was journaling as if I were coaching you.

The first piece of advice that I have for you is to be prepared. Grief takes a tremendous toll on your physical body. Your energy will wax and wane. You may experience aches and pains that seem to have no rhyme or reason to them. So, with that in mind, the first consideration as you begin the healing process is to adopt some of the attitudes and strategies of an expectant mother and give extra special attention to the care and nurturing of your physical body.

While you may not be able to sleep, try to get plenty of rest and eat foods that nourish you.

You may not feel like it, but it is so helpful to get fresh air and exercise daily; even if it means walking to the neighbors mailbox and back today and then two mailboxes away and back the next day. Movement will help release stress and the stress hormone cortisol, as well as create the happy endorphins.

Just as the expectant mother immediately schedules monthly visits with her doctor, it might be good for you to arrange for regular visits with a therapist, coach, counselor, clergy member or trusted friend.

While prenatal care is focused on the physical body, grief care has a huge component of emotional care needed. There are many specialists who have devoted their lives to supporting you through grief. It is prudent to find the right helper as soon as possible. You do NOT need to go through this alone.

Caution is advised in the use of drugs or alcohol. The pain can become so overwhelming that you may just want to run away. Many of my clients tell me that drinking to ease the pain was the worst mistake they ever made.

Without exception, they say that once the numbness wears off the pain seems ten times worse than it was before. They are, therefore, inclined to drink more and longer; eventually unable to stop.

Drinking, drugs, overworking; whatever you might be tempted to use to escape the pain are what I call "destructive habits of distraction." You can only distract yourself for so long before your mind and body will no longer allow it. Unfortunately, many people have discovered that by trying to ignore or distract themselves from the pain instead of learning to deal with and heal it, they experience physical diseases as a result of their unaddressed grief.

In pregnancy, special vitamins are prescribed. In grief, antidepressants may offer necessary support. The question you might ask yourself is whether or not you can use the medical support without guilt or shame.

If, for example, you had a broken leg, no one would blame or judge you for getting the necessary support for the healing of the leg. Remember, however, that a cast is a temporary support and no one would ever plan to live with the cast forever. A wise doctor will both support and monitor your use of medications.

Because the physical stress drains the body, the mental capacities are affected. Almost immediately you might experience incredibly foggy thinking, forgetfulness, and mood swings. Patience is always a virtue, but we generally think of that as being offered to others. This is the time I nudge my clients to cut themselves some slack! Can you be patient with and forgive **yourself** as you travel along on your very personal healing journey?

You may be surprised or annoyed to learn how eager your family, friends - and even complete strangers - are to share their life stories of trauma and loss. It may seem that everyone has advice for you. Your experience makes you part of a unique club. Understand that because you are feeling so raw and vulnerable, it may be easy to feel offended when others share their stories.

Your EGO mind will say "No, you do NOT understand." Holding your tongue at times like that can be challenging. I suggest that you write down the things that people say to you that are most hurtful in the moment. Work with your coach, therapist or clergy member to try and release the bitterness that can take root from such conversations.

Just as the first signs of pregnancy are often accompanied by bouts of morning sickness, don't be surprised if mornings are the worst! Something seems to happen during the night, either chemically or mentally. It is pretty common to find that the first hours of the day are toughest. As you get moving though, your energy, mood and physical pains do subside.

I discovered what I call the "Don't Blink, Don't Think" responses to waking. Instead of lying in the bed letting my ego voices strike up the mourning parade, I would begin instantly affirming every good thing I could think of and get my feet on the floor as quickly as possible. At least for me, this created a new pattern of waking feeling more hopeful and more able to find a reason to get out of the bed in the morning.

For some measure of time, it will seem that everything reminds you of your trauma and loss; a song, a scent, a location. Everything seems to trigger another set of memories and another layer of grieving. Again, I implore you to try to be patient with yourself and your process.

I began setting aside time each day to focus on my grief. I decided that just as an expecting mother would go about her business, do her job and work on preparing for her baby after hours, I would take the same approach. It was amazingly helpful. My heart, mind and body knew there would be time each day for grieving and my little EGO mind knew it could not hijack my thinking 24/7.

Believe it or not, the time will come when you find that you have processed the majority of the memories, answered the antagonizing questions and have begun to settle into a new normal for your life.

Remember that just as pregnancy and raising a child is a process, grief is a process. Life will never be exactly the same as it was before, but you will create a new life and a new normal.

If your trauma involves any loss of a sense of safety and predictability in the world, Tapping can help in hours, not months. One of the fabulous gifts of Tapping is that a skilled practitioner can not only help you relieve the sad and fearful feelings, they can also help you gain new perspectives and insights about your journey and, yes, the gifts and opportunities that can be found in change.

If you're grieving the loss of a loved one, you and I both know that no one can take their place. The objective is not to replace them, but to remember them and to honor them in a way that celebrates their life and supports your own.

What, if anything, would it profit you or the deceased for you to remain forever in a state of grief?

The reality is that life is an ongoing process. You will experience more contrasting experiences of joy and sorrow until the day that you, too, pass.

Robert Frost was quoted as saying, "In three words I can sum up life; it goes on."

As with the expectant mother, you may find that you will feel differently from day-to-day and even from moment-to-moment. You may have one good day followed by several bad days; whatever that might mean for you. It is impossible to predict these changes in your emotional weather, but remember that even on the stormiest of days the sun is always there just behind the clouds.

I affectionately call these closet days. Just tell your family and friends that you are cleaning out another emotional closet and that you need time to sort through some things.

Ask them to support you in whatever way you need them to. Would it help if they sit with you? Do you not want anyone to even look at you? What if they could drop off lunch or dinner and just leave it in the refrigerator for you?

Your first reaction to this idea may be resistance and you might be thinking, "I don't want to put them out." I would invite you to put yourself in their place for a moment. Can you imagine how helpless they are feeling watching you suffer and struggle and how they feel that they have little or nothing they can do to make *you* feel better? Giving them clear and simple tasks that are specific to meet your needs will actually be a gift to them.

When you choose to focus on appreciation for the good days and try not to begrudge the bad days, you will feel better all the way around. Remember, to all things there is indeed a time and a season and even your grief and loss can give way to new life and a renewed sense of purpose.

The bottom line, my friend, is that in any trauma, loss or change, the only way to do it is to go through it!

Grief Is . . . Left Over Love

You weren't through loving them yet and now you may feel as if you will choke on all of the feelings that are left over and trapped inside of you.

The smell of hospital permeated everything. The gown I was wearing - though I have no idea why they call it a gown; it is a cape at best and a nightmare for those of us who are eternally modest - the walls, the bedding, everything had that trademark scent. It is as if they put everything through an autoclave and remove all hint of life.

The little hospital room was quiet with the exception of the beep-beep-beep of the heart monitor. The numbers flashed in an accusatory rhythm; 178-175-177-169. Clearly my heart rate was too high. The three nurses shuffled around me; the one standing at my side watching my every expression as if she was expecting a major meltdown. The other two fiddled with equipment and did paperwork. One might occasionally step out of the room only to reappear without bidding.

Perspiration began to run down my temple and drip onto my gown.

We were waiting for the doctor.

I was panting now. I kept willing myself to hang on. Just a little longer. But the little voice in my head was filled with alarm. It said "I can't – I can't – I can't" at least a dozen times before I surrendered and said it out loud.

"I can't" I bleated, gasping to catch my breath, "go any longer."

The nurse that had been staring me down put a hand on my bicep and said, "Okay, try and slow to a walk; don't stop too quickly, okay?"

I slowed my pace on the treadmill to a walk as quickly as I could, feeling nauseous and exhausted. My calves were burning. I could not seem to breathe in enough oxygen. My heart pounded in my chest like a base drum. Finally, the numbers on the monitor slowed to 160---155---148. Wow, I thought. I know that my maximum target heart rate must be around 130. I was above the threshold for nearly 12 minutes.

My feelings of accomplishment were swiftly dashed. The doctor bolted through the door looking impatient and perturbed. She grabbed the strip of paper that exuded from the heart monitor machine, clicked her pen and made a couple of marks on the paper strip as she swiftly ran her thumbs from mid-point on the page to the end of the strip.

"Your heart is fine but you should be in much better shape for your age. You need to get more exercise," she said with a disgusted smirk. She signed a form and left as abruptly as she came in.

I didn't catch her name. Clearly I was just another dolt on her rounds today. "I didn't ask for this stress test!" I thought. "Thanks for nothing" the ego voice in my head yelled after her. Fortunately, the nurse that had been attending me through the day had taken the time to understand why I was here and had heard my story. His face was filled with compassion.

"Don't let it get to you. You'll get your strength back." He said as he nodded encouragingly.

I sat in the car and cried for ten minutes before I left the hospital parking lot.

It had been several months since my son had died. Because of my long family history of heart conditions my doctor ordered a stress test to ensure that the constant chest pain I had been having was only emotional and not physical. At least now I knew she was right. Good news, I suppose, but the pain lingered.

After this lovely day at the hospital I was eager to figure out what was really happening in my body. Why would grief...how could grief, an emotion, cause such a strong physical pain? Certainly I had felt emotional pain before, but this was over the top. Having always been very empathetic, I was accustomed to being called sensitive and, more often than not, too sensitive. I had experienced hurts and disappointments in the past that left my heart feeling bruised, but I guess losing a child had actually caused what I had heard referred to as an emotional heart break.

I was haunted by the question, "Why does it hurt so much?" It became my constant companion and was like a little brown mouse living in my pocket. The question gnawed at me night and day. When I would step into the shower, its little head would pop up. When I would shut down my computer at the end of the day, oh, there it was. The first thing in the morning when my hand intuitively reached for my aching chest it would scamper brazenly across my mind. I could almost feel the question staring at me; glaring, daring me to know the answer.

And then one day, in the middle of a couple's session, I caught it!

They were the last session of the day. Carrie and Rod had been married for about seven years and they were really struggling with intimacy. Bottom line, Carrie was hurt and angry all the time and Rod wanted more physical connection. She was not having it, so they were at a stalemate.

After the obligatory small talk and a round of generic tapping to get the resistances down I asked, "Carrie, can you tell me about a time in the past when Rod did or didn't do something that really hurt your feelings and is still popping into your mind when you are upset with him now?"

"Oh, yes!" she said, without skipping a beat, "When we went on our family vacation." As she spoke her countenance clouded. She sat back on the couch, crossed her arms and pursed her lips as she recited the whole story in fine detail about how he had chosen to go fishing and biking and hiking all weekend with his brother and cousins and left her in a cabin with a sick baby and in-laws that she felt didn't like her. Clearly she felt betrayed, left out and hurt.

"Oh, here we go again" Rod chimed in, adding his own animated posturing. He threw the weight of his upper body into the back of the couch, put one hand up and shielded his eyes as he wagged his head from side to side in an over-exaggerated "no."

"Okay!" I said, with a little giggle. "I think we have something to work with now!"

"Carrie, how long ago was that little camping trip?"

"Three years ago."

"Hmm; and yet, when you tell me the story today, how long ago does it…*FEEL*?"

"Oh, it feels like it was yesterday."

I tried to ignore Rod's look of despair and turned to ask him, "Rod, whenever the two of you have an argument or a disagreement, how many of these types of stories does she bring up from your past?"

Rod looked at me with a hint of vindication in his smirk. "Dozens!" he said passionately.

"Great!" I celebrated with a great big smile. "That tells me she still loves you!"

His look countered that idea, but I rushed ahead and started coaching:

"Whenever we start a mutually loving relationship, both parties are enamored and happy to be together. Our hearts and minds are wide open (I held my right hand straight out in front of me, palm up and fingers stretched wide open). And when we have a disagreement or someone says something hurtful, it's like dropping a brick on us (I punctuated the idea using my left hand to represent the brick dropping into the open hand, causing it to close and drop). We cannot help but close up because it hurt us and our first response is to retract and withdraw. Does this sound about right to you guys?"

They both nodded yes.

"In a new relationship, the first time our friend or lover drops an emotional brick on us we generally get our spirits back open pretty quickly. The second time, we are little more hesitant to open back up to them and so on and so forth. Each of those bricks begins to build what we would call our emotional wall. The longer each brick is left unaddressed, the more likely the relationship will suffer and possibly, end. Rod, as long as Carrie is still showing you the bricks when she is feeling angry and hurt, she is still IN. She loves you enough to trust you to try and help her remove the bricks from her heart and help her tear down the wall.

But, you need to beware! If these bricks - the hurtful incidents - are not healed, pretty soon there are less and less emotional and physical connections and, before you know it, she doesn't want you to touch her. She doesn't care anymore. She will just want you to go away. She will give up."

I shrugged my shoulders to emphasize the point.

"I cannot tell you how many couples I've had sit in my office as a last ditch effort to save their marriage. If one, or both, of them have a 20-foot tall emotional wall and they are not willing to open up and talk through these stories (often they have forgotten the story behind the bricks in the wall), there is not a lot I can do for them.

Rod, can we agree that with this new information, it is actually good news that Carrie is still bringing up the story about the cabin?"

He half-heartedly nodded, yes.

You may not realize it, Rod, but you have one of two choices in that moment. You can go with the ego reaction and jump into what I call Emotional A.D.D. (Attack, Defend and Deny) and refuse to talk about it or you can quiet your ego voice and try to stay fully present with her in her pain. I can teach you how to listen with your heart.

I submit to you that each of those stories are remnants of unfinished business which Carrie is begging for you to look at with her so she can truly open up to you and feel safe to trust you again."

Carrie gasped. "That is exactly what it feels like! He wants me to feel romantic and intimate, but I cannot bring myself to hardly let him touch me. I don't think he cares how much he has hurt me!" She said as her hands flew up to cover her face as she began to cry.

Rod leaned forward to try to comfort her.

I coached them through several rounds of tapping and reflective listening. It's not easy to stay open when you are feeling resentful. Likewise, it is challenging to sit and listen to someone share how much you have hurt them without feeling ashamed and guilty and trying to explain yourself and offer excuses. They both took the coaching well and I was especially proud of Rod for hanging in and hearing and validating her pain, round after round.

As the session drew to a close I asked Carrie for a little feedback. She was talking again and she said she felt more hopeful than she had in years. She even let Rod hold her hand. It seemed that her spirit was starting to open again, if only a little crack.

Rod was beginning to understand that when Carrie was bringing up the past, she <u>wasn't</u> trying to make him feel ashamed. She <u>wasn't</u> trying to make him suffer. She <u>was</u> trying to connect with him emotionally. All Carrie wanted was to feel like he really "got it." She yearned to know that he was "feeling her pain" and that once he understood, all it took was for him to communicate his pain at having hurt her that way. He had never wanted to hurt her. The emotional walls were beginning to crumble.

As I hugged them goodbye, Carrie had a little smile on her face and Rod's voice was soft and gentle. I giggled to myself as I wondered if he was glad that he was leaving with all of his male parts intact.

I was surprised by something that occurred to me during that session. You see, I've been teaching the concept of open and closed spirits for years. I was fully aware that a closed spirit always elicits a physical feeling - generally, it's a feeling of sadness or depression. A closed spirit hurts.

"That's it!" I thought. That morning at the hospital when I got the awful news about Devin's death, my spirit, my mind, my heart, slammed shut! (I think I even heard the thud.) By having such a strong, resistant reaction to the news of my son, I had closed off all of the normal flow of energy in my spirit and heart. No wonder the pain was so excruciating!

My heart-ache was an emotional brick of sorrow. I was hurting on a soul level. As I reflected on Carrie and how willing and eager she was to be understood, I became aware of my own subconscious ego belief that I could not heal because no one could understand how much it hurt to lose my baby boy.

My heart, it seemed, was closed for the foreseeable future.

I decided to devote a few minutes each day to my hurting heart. I would tap on the phrases as they came up; starting with the idea that "no one could understand" and after several very tearful rounds I felt genuinely ready to add, "And I don't need them to understand. After all, what would their understanding change about the situation anyway?"

Then I would consciously focus on extending love and joy from my heart as I went throughout my day. Smiles and love to the little girl on the elevator or the man at the grocery store. Each day I would coach myself to extend some of that leftover love that had been all wadded up inside my heart. After all, I thought, holding onto it isn't doing anyone any good.

I began a ritual of counting my blessings and I redirected my thoughts toward areas where there was love and joy in my life. Eventually, these happy thoughts began to include celebrating the lovely memories I had of my son. Wouldn't it be wonderful, I thought to myself, if every time I remember him, hear his name, see his guitar or see a picture of him, I don't burst out in tears, but I burst into a smile and beam with love? I was making progress.

Over time, the pain eased. The conscious focusing worked. The heartache diminished, little by little. And one day I realized...the pain was gone.

Statistics show that for up to five years after a major trauma or loss and grief, there is an exponential increase in the number of physical pains, illnesses and even chronic diseases. It makes perfect sense to me that when we react by resisting and closing our spirits; we are blocking our own healthy flow of life energy.

I was with a 56-year old client of mine that mentioned - off handedly - that it was about time for her yearly bout of bronchitis. I was curious about why this was such a strong belief for her so I asked her a few questions, including how long this "expecting bronchitis" had been a pattern for her. She had to think about it for a minute or two, but sure enough she tracked it back to the year that her marriage ended. When I suggested that her bronchitis was a symptom of unresolved grief, the proverbial light bulb went on over her head. For the next three weeks we devoted each of our hourly sessions to clearing all the aspects of grief around her failed marriage, breaking up her family, perceived failure by divorce and the many resentments and struggles she had survived as a single mom.

Just prior to her fourth session she phoned me. She was obviously in tears but these were happy tears. She was calling to express her amazement and her gratitude. She said she could not remember the last time she was able to breathe so deeply. And, yes, she skipped her expected bout of bronchitis for the first time in years. We had uprooted the emotional trauma. Her heart and spirit were open again. Not only did her health return, but she quickly manifested a new romance and an increase in her salary! Cool!

What might be some clues that your spirit is open? Think about when you are really happy, when you are having one of those days when everything is going great; all green lights and empty parking spaces when you need them and everyone is friendly. These are all reflections of an open and in-the-flow spirit.

What feelings might be symptoms of a closed spirit? Simply stated, the opposites of all the above; feeling antisocial, boredom or detachment from life, pre-occupation with sorrow or life problems and, yes, whining!

A closed spirit is what I refer to as P.R. or Persistent Resistance. When you are in P.R. it is like everything pushes your metaphorical buttons. The unconscious reaction is to say no, to everything!

With a closed spirit, your mind is closed and you become un-teachable. With a closed spirit, you cannot receive love thus you have made yourself un-loveable. Your resistance determines not only what you can give, but what you can receive. While it seems counter-intuitive to be open when you feel the most vulnerable and raw, I propose that consciously being open is the FASTEST way to heal your grief on all levels.

Try on the idea of seeking out ways to open your heart and spirit. Give love, acceptance and understanding instead of waiting for someone to give it to you. You may be pleasantly surprised at what will manifest in your life.

Jan Luther

Grief Is . . . A Magician

It can make old friends disappear and turn complete strangers into soul mates.

It was mid-morning. My sisters and I were in the kitchen standing around the center island discussing the small gathering I had planned for the night after the funeral. The doorbell rang as we were talking:

"What do you want to feed them?" one sister asked.

"I think we could just set out several appetizers and be fine," I answered.

We all stopped speaking as a woman appeared from around the corner. She was carrying a large foil covered pan out in front of her, an oven mitt on each hand; she marched right up to our little circle.

"Can I set these here?" She asked as she motioned toward the island with a nod of her head.

"Uh, sure," I answered as I quickly retrieved a couple of trivets from the drawer and placed them on the counter.

"I'll be right back, I have one more." She did an about face and headed back toward the front door.

I looked at my daughter inquisitively. "Do you know her?" I whispered, thinking maybe she was the mother of one of her friends.

"Uh, no," she said with a furrowed eyebrow and half smile. "I thought you did." We grinned at each other curiously and shrugged our shoulders.

The woman quickly returned, as promised, with a second equally large pan which she placed on the second trivet.

After a quick glance at my sisters I realized I needed to say something.

"Forgive, me" I said sheepishly, "Have we met?"

"No." She said, matter-of-factly and stated her name. "I live down the street. When I heard the news about your son, I just had to do something." She took a breath, turned to my sister and said, "These are lasagnas," and quickly gave instructions for reheating the two large pans of pasta.

Surprised and humbled at her graciousness, I said "Thank-you, so much."

She simply dipped her head and quietly said, "I am so sorry for your loss" and she disappeared down the hallway without any fanfare.

My sisters and I exchanged glances, looked at the huge pans of food and with a big smile and giggle, one of them said, "Problem solved."

I did serve my friends that yummy lasagna for our gathering. And we had a bit left over for lunch the next day. It was as if this woman heard us fretting over what to serve and angelically appeared to answer our prayer.

This was one of the many, many acts of service our family received when my son died; from dozens of people, many of whom we had never even met.

On the morning Devin died, my husband had called his sisters soon after we returned from the hospital. By that evening, several ladies from their neighborhood showed up at our door with food, drinks and paper plates and cups to help us feed all of our guests. These, too, were people we had never met before; magically appearing in our time of need. These wonderful souls have gone from strangers to friends whom we will forever be indebted to for their acts of kindness.

Ironically, many people that I had considered to be my friends were painfully absent during that time. Some of them remained absent for years. Occasionally, I would bump into an old friend after the funeral and they would mumble something about "wanted to give you space" or "I was trusting that you would call me if you needed anything." It often left me wondering what fear or pain my situation brought up for them that caused them to avoid contacting me.

Sometimes people would slink away and avoid addressing me or having any conversation. I would often jest with my family that it was as if some folks were afraid that my experience was contagious. Often, the condolences were shrouded in the deep fears that seeing me in my situation brought up for them. I learned quickly not to take it personally.

Of course, there were times that first year or so when I would meet a friend or acquaintance and have to break the news to them. It wasn't long before I began to weigh the options of whether to tell them or not based upon how close we were. You might say that it becomes a matter of deciding, do they "need to know."

If our meeting was at a local market and fleeting, I often decided to not even bring it up. On the other hand, if I met a parent or friend of Devin's I always tried to share the news as gently as I could. Needless to say, it was a relief when that second and third year rolled around and it seemed everyone that needed to know, knew.

After the flurry of activity that accompanies our initial life-changing experience, people will, of course, go about their day-to-day lives. It is easy to feel like they have forgotten you and your challenges. Inevitably, the temptation will arise to feel unloved and forgotten. That little ego voice can be a real demon sometimes. I mean, really. Just when you need peace of mind the most, that little voice can show up with some of the most hurtful and hateful thinking patterns ever.

Another trauma that may have delayed grief is when one is diagnosed with a life-changing illness. If this is true for you, your first hurdle may not be the disease itself, but the little ego voices that will march in and set up camp in your head. Left unchecked, they will begin to prophesy a dreadful future. If you do not stand up to them, they will whisper morning, noon and night about how sad it all is, how unfair, how hopeless. If you do not thwart them, long before you are truly suffering physically, you can be emotionally and spiritually dying inside. Before your symptoms become disabling, your negative thinking can disable you!

Regardless of what your trauma or loss is, I challenge you to take an hour and really watch your thinking.

Are your thoughts directed toward taking action, living large and making the most of every day or are you allowing yourself to dwell on the Persistent Resistance phrases like:

- What will I do now?
- How could this be?
- This wasn't supposed to happen to me.
- I did everything right.
- This isn't fair.
- I don't want to do this.

Any time you feel your energy dropping and your mood turning sour, take two minutes and write down the most recent self-talk from your ego. Once you have sifted out the feelings, capture the key phrases and tap on them. Use a set of simple reframes like: *these are just feelings, feelings are not truth*, and *feelings are ever-changing*.

Your health and happiness depend upon you making the connection that your feelings are always based upon what you are thinking.

Here is a quick example of what I might tap on with you to challenge the negative belief that it is hopeless:

"Even though I am feeling hopeless, I deeply and completely accept this feeling. I want to remember that it **is** just a feeling. I am open to feeling better."

"Even though I am thinking about how hopeless I am feeling, I deeply and completely love and accept myself - even when I choose to think about feeling hopeless - and I am willing to change my thinking."

"Even though hopeless is such a dreary word and I am not sure why I would want to dwell on something so dreary, I deeply and completely love and accept myself and I recognize that I have the power to choose how I feel by choosing what I think."

Over time, if you can learn to catch your negative thoughts and maybe even say to yourself, "Oh, so that is how I am feeling about that today. Okay." And if you can tap and breathe for 90 seconds, that emotion will rise up and then fade away when you do not feed it with your attention.

A simple question to always ask yourself is: "What kind of day will I have if I dwell on this thought?"

As you become far less tolerant of your negative thinking, you will quickly find that you are able to go about your day without suffering a rollercoaster of emotions.

You may be surprised by how the simple act of observing your feelings can reduce their power over you. It has been my experience that by neither resisting nor agreeing with the feelings - simply observing them - they can melt away; literally in less than two minutes.

When dealing with your friends and acquaintances, be mindful that they are now seeing you in a different light. They may have never met the vulnerable or the grieving you. Meeting you in your new role automatically puts them in a new role. They need some time to figure out how to interact with you and the changes.

If your family member or friend is very close to you, it may be unbearable for them to see you in such pain. It may be that they are not equipped with the skills to offer comfort or counsel. They may decide they cannot be with you in your process; try not to take that personally. It may actually be best in the long run for them to exit for a while instead of creating more pain by behaving or speaking in ways that would only add to your distress.

Another challenge I have seen clients struggle with is what we might think of as the "crystal ball" mentality. Are you imagining that someone close to you should know what to do or say or that they should automatically know what you need? Tempting, right? Ego will say, "If they love me, they would, or will…" Remember that no matter how well someone knows you, they cannot read your mind.

Your friends and loved ones will most likely be walking on eggshells around you, trying to be extra careful not to upset you. Sometimes it will be tempting to think that it will be easier to just stop being out or around people all together.

Instead of avoiding your friends or social groups, I would encourage you to participate in the activities you find meaningful; more fully now than ever. Being out and active will help allay some of the little ego temptations to dwell on your situation.

It is good to prepare for your encounters before you go out. Consider, for example, the fears that your friends may be struggling with. There will be some in the group that have no idea how to interact with you. They will be waiting for some verbal or emotional clues from you. Are they supposed to pretend that nothing has changed or do you want them to talk about things openly with you?

It will save everyone - especially you - a lot of time and distress if you can clearly define and express how you are feeling and how you would like them to act around you.

I found this particularly helpful with one of my own spiritual study groups. A few weeks after my son died, I returned to the group for the first time and intentionally invited everyone to talk about his death. I answered a few questions and shared a couple of stories about some of the amazing synchronicities and miracles I had experienced along the journey. It was my intention to alleviate their fears and inspire and comfort them.

During the evening, I passed around some of my special little keepsakes, including the little blue pouch that the state patrolman had given me at the hospital with my son's wallet and personal belongings. It was moving to see how respectful everyone was; the way they handled my treasures, the tone of reverence they had in their questions and comments.

Just to be sure that I had cleared up any remaining fears they might have, I told them that I would always be open to talking about Devin and the accident. I wanted them to realize that I was not so fragile that the topic was off limits.

There were several audible sighs from the attendees throughout that evening and, all in all, I left feeling very comforted and closer to them than ever.

Remember, too, that if you would like greeting cards or phone calls or someone to stop by and visit, you may need to ask for such things. Neighbors, family members or friends will inevitably ask what they can do to help. Why not let them know what would encourage and support you?

Everyone will appreciate clear direction from you. Just the act of clarifying for yourself what you do and don't want will give you an added sense of stability and empowerment.

If you need to cry, cry. Be prepared that crying automatically brings out the comforter in some people and the stifle-er in others. Some people simply cannot seem to cope with anyone in tears. If you can clearly state that you may cry and then tell them if you do or do not want a tissue or a hug, etc., it may be a great healing opportunity for those that struggle with what to do when someone shows strong emotions. You will also find that by coming to agreements ahead of time, it actually liberates you to be real with your feelings at any given time.

In highly emotional situations, grieving people are naturally protective of their own feelings first. You may be closing off without realizing it. In doing so you may not realize that you have inadvertently said or done something that has offended someone else.

While you might think that it is unfair or unreasonable that someone would not forgive you for such an offense at such a vulnerable time, remember that it can and does happen and you will need to choose how to respond or react to the hurt feelings of others.

I find that grief offers ample opportunities to step outside of your comfort zone. You may be given opportunities to learn to forgive, over and over. Or you may be given the opportunity to learn to be humble and to receive graciously.

If your story is one of a lost loved one, you may meet someone new on your journey who had been very close to your deceased loved one. This can be unsettling to your ego voice. It does not like to feel left out. The idea that you are missing your loved one and that this person has connections to a "part of them" that you cannot get to can create an enormous mental and emotional tug-of-war. Do you want to hear all about their relationship? Or, do you want them to go away?

What may be most helpful is to request an open door for later. There may come a time later in your process when you are feeling stronger and would like to ask questions and know more about their relationship. Most people welcome the opportunity to reminisce.

You may have neighbors, relatives or distant friends who suddenly appear out of nowhere.

My client, Kara, had been raised by her single mother since she was about eight years old. She knew that her father had remarried and had two daughters with his second wife. After Kara's father died, one of her half-sisters began to email her regularly. She said she wanted to get to know Kara. Kara was hesitant and cautious.

In our first session, Kara and I worked through the first three aspects of grief. She was shocked when her parents separated. She was angry that her father didn't fight to keep her. As we tapped along, she realized that she had been imagining that her step-sisters had been living the perfect life with a perfect father-daughter relationship. She had created a "fantasy father" in her mind. She had been jealous of her step-sister her whole life. Her resistance to meeting with her began to melt away as we came to the awareness that Kara could certainly show up and be present and decide how much or how little of herself she would share; or how much contact she would commit to in the future with her step-sister.

After their meeting Kara humbly reported that her step-sister had been very gracious. In fact, she had regaled her with story after story of how mean and unloving her father had actually been to her. It turned out that living with the father was much more painful than living without him. Kara had great compassion for her step-sister and the jealousy melted away. They connected on a new level.

Your challenge may be friends or neighbors that seem to want to insert themselves in your business. Your ego might tout, "Who do they think they are?" This may be protective or it may be blocking an opportunity to receive love and support.

If you are clear that you really do not want them in your space, it may require some tact, but stating what you need and want is not that difficult. Tell them what you would like them to do (or not to do) very specifically.

For example: "Thank you, Betty, for taking time out of your day to call me (or come and sit with me). I am not in a mood to have company right now. I will call you if I decide later that I would like your company."

Don't feel obligated to offer excuses; no timeline, and no commitment. Being firm and clear will set a no-nonsense tone and you will feel empowered and safe to have your heart open.

Gifts and cards often come flowing in. You will have to decide if you will send thank-you cards for the many acts of kindness.

One of my clients shared with me that after her husband died there was so much to do that the only way she could allay her guilty feelings of not being able to personally respond to all the kind calls, notes and visits she had received was to create a simple form letter:

Dear _____,

Thank you for your call, card, gift or visit.

Your expression of condolence is deeply appreciated. You can visit (deceased name) at the (cemetery location). Should you wish to make an honorarium, please do so by sending your gift to (name of charity).

With gratitude,
-signature-

I was proud of her for her creative solution. I was surprised when I heard that some folks had chosen to be offended by this. We tapped on the realization that this was yet another example of how judgments close the mind and spirit. We tapped on allowing them to be judgmental and to be proud of her for making the time to respond to every single card and letter in record time.

Our long-held opinions soon become our beliefs, whether they are based in truth or not.

Our beliefs then become our subconscious rules about life.

These rules dictate your life - whether you are aware of them or not.

How can you spot an unwritten rule from your book of beliefs? Listen for the "should."

Jan Luther

Grief Is . . .Watching someone else's life flash before your eyes.

From the moment you learn of their passing, every thought seems to be filled with memories of the loved one.

I rubbed my hands together briskly to get the lotion to soak into my skin. It was almost time for my next client. I lifted the tissue box and gave it a little shake as I peered in to see how full it was. The little basket that holds the bottles of water for my clients was full. The thermostat was set at 72 and I adjusted the dimmer switch to reduce the glare of the overhead chandelier just a bit. I always want my clients to feel comforted and comfortable in my office.

I saw Keisha's car pull up and so I went out the front door to greet her.

Her eyes were red, her cheeks streaked with mascara and she literally ran toward me and threw her arms around my neck.

"Oh, Jan, I just don't know what to do with myself. I cannot keep it together. I had to leave work yesterday and today. I just don't think I can bear another day."

I hugged her tightly and consciously sent her love and energy. One arm around her waist, I ushered her into my office and helped her get situated on the couch.

Her pain came gushing out in a 10-minute rant. Sometimes I couldn't really make out what she was saying. I just listened and gave her my full loving attention. Her tears and snot and despair went into the tissues which went into the trash can, one after another. We tapped and sighed and by the end of our hour together, Keisha was sitting taller, speaking more clearly; her countenance and her conversation much lighter. The hugs on the way out the door were filled with love and gratitude.

This work is not for the faint of heart. Every day I have the privilege of helping my clients make sense of the insanity that life has handed them. And there is nothing that makes one feel more insane than grief.

It begins from the moment you receive the dreadful news that your job or finances, your health or your loved one is gone. Shock, confusion; it's as if your brain gets scrambled when things change so abruptly.

It is hard to comprehend that something could be one way for months or years and then, in one moment, change completely. Life generally offers us change in small, manageable bites. Trauma and death bring a change so sudden that the mind has to reboot.

When you get the news, if you are not saying it audibly you are probably thinking it silently: "But, I just saw them" or "But, it was supposed to be a regular doctor visit." Or "But, we were just making plans." It is easy for our mind to lock up, like our computers do when there is an overload of information to process.

I like to draw the analogy that each memory is a file folder that has recorded everything that you experienced emotionally, spiritually, mentally and physically in every moment of every story. What did you see, hear, smell and feel - emotionally and physically?

These mental files create the proverbial "box" that we each live in. The walls of our box make us feel safe. They are the parameters that make life feel predictable and manageable for us. When someone delivers dreadful news, it's as if they have taken a sledge hammer to one of our walls.

Our little ego mind turns on all the lights and begins to rifle through all of our mental files, looking both for evidence to argue against it and searching cautiously for proof of the truth. We run the mental movies from our past experiences that, of course, feel like it was yesterday. Some of us may be tempted to resist the news and obstinately play the old movies over and over in defiance and denial. We each cope with shock and trauma in our own way and in our own time.

When you lose a loved one, this phenomenon is played out very clearly as friends and family gather together, each describing their mental movies to one another.

Each person is processing their loss by revisiting the person in their own mind. Often, the person being honored seems as unique and individual as the people sharing the stories. Don't be surprised if you or a loved one gets triggered by some of the personal stories that others share. It is useless to argue with others and their movies.

When Patty's oldest son died, she had to face her estranged daughter-in-law, Emily. It wasn't long after the funeral that each woman – racked with grief – began talking to extended family members, each behind the other's back. Emily was telling everyone how her husband had chosen to avoid the family for years because, in her words, "they had used and abused him."

Patty, equally distraught, told stories about how her daughter-in-law had been a lazy hypochondriac that sucked the life out of her son.

Faced with the dilemma of choosing sides, the family suffered tremendously.

Why would they do this? The insight that came to me was that they were both so desperate to capture and hold onto their own personal relationship with the man that they simply could not imagine that he could have loved them both.

Maybe they were crying out for validation. Perhaps their ego voice was saying: "I loved him best" or "He loved me the most."

It was so sad and seemed so unnecessary.

No matter what your relationship to the person or situation, your experience will be yours and yours alone. We cannot compare them because they are so personal and unique. I assure you that if you have lost a loved one, they loved you like they did not love anyone else.

That is the nature of relationships; every relationship is truly one of a kind. It is not helpful to compete or compare your loss and pain with others.

Supporting others and allowing them to share their own memories and pain of loss will help you maintain an open heart and mind and bring you much needed healing peace.

In the early stages of grief, since all the lights are on in your mental filing cabinets, you may find that that you feel you are trapped in your mental "movie theater." From the moment you awaken in the morning (if you do manage to go to sleep) until you crumple in the bed again at night, your mind may be playing bits and pieces of memories like mini-movies starring your loss or lost loved one.

While these movies generally begin with the last experience when things were normal, you will find that the stories will randomly jump from past to future, from happy to sad and - all too frequently - the movie will stick on some painful past memory about which you feel guilt or regret.

When you are confronted with these painful memories, recognize them as another ego temptation to close your spirit and isolate you by feeding on guilt or regrets.

With every relationship there are ups and downs. Some are seemingly lopsided, being either more positive or more negative. Over time, we often come to realize that the most challenging relationships are the ones that forced us to grow the most.

If you have regrets or memories of mistakes from the past, don't avoid them. Address them. Zero in on the ego's accusation:

> *I did (or did not) say or do (what) to whom and I feel (what) about that now.*

By applying tapping on just that phrase, you can tremendously reduce the distressing emotions. And, better still, tapping a simple initial phrase like this will automatically invite your ego mind to start popping up equally distressing thoughts and beliefs for tapping.

Let me give you a very simple example of how I might use tapping to reduce the distress on the very common regret of "not doing enough" for someone who has passed. Even if this is not a fitting phrase for you, notice that as you read along, the little ego voice will play what I call the boomerang game with you. You say one thing and the ego mind tosses up other accusatory thoughts and memories, one after the other.

"Even though I am full of grief and I cannot seem to shake these memories of all the things I did NOT do for my loved one, I deeply and completely love and accept myself.

Clearly I love them or I would not feel so guilty.

Even though I cannot seem to stop thinking about all those times when I think I didn't do enough for my loved one and it causes me great heartache, I deeply and completely love and accept that maybe I could have done more.

102

Maybe I could have done better. Still, I would like to release this guilt and pain.

No amount of regret or pain will bring them back or give me a second chance.

Even though this regret and guilt merely amplify my pain, my little ego voice must have some objective in keeping me focused on what I did NOT do.

I would like to consider that while I certainly could have done more, perhaps if I celebrate the things I was able to do I can begin healing my broken heart now.

- *What did I do right and well?*
- *What, if anything, did I NOT do that would have hurt them?*
- *Did I actually have the intention of causing them to suffer?*
- *Is it possible that I was emotionally empty and giving all that I could at the time?*
- *Could I be willing to forgive myself?*
- *Is it possible that because I could not save them or that I cannot have a "do-over" that I might <u>never</u> <u>feel</u> like I did enough?"*

(I have more information on using this technique that I call **"The Boomerang Game"** on my web site. You can receive the free training by registering for my newsletter at <u>TheEGOTamer.com</u>).

Could you consider letting the guilt and regret go? Could you consider forgiving others if that is the problem? Every choice will lead you along the path to more of <u>the same feelings you are focused on</u> in any given moment.

If you choose to be sad, stuck, angry or regretting you will continue to travel the path of sadness and guilt. If you can choose to accept that at any moment in our lives we are all doing the best we can under the circumstances, compassion, patience and love will guide your journey. Most of us discover that we are literally receiving the energy, emotion and experience we have been extending to others.

I personally have come to the conclusion that what we call Karma is simply the opportunity to choose again. If for any reason I am dissatisfied and, therefore, holding a judgment against myself, a person or situation, it will keep showing up for me until I decide that it just "is what it is" and I choose to release any of my remaining beliefs and "shoulds" about it. Sounds simple, I know. But, isn't it wonderful that we have the power to choose again?

My client, Sophia, wanted to choose to heal her grief. She was doing all she knew how to do to get over the loss of her young husband. She was all too familiar with the mental movies. She had made some great progress working with her therapist. Wisely, the counselor encouraged her to focus on the "good and happy times." This worked wonders for a short time and then her little ego voice turned on her.

Every time she did remember a happy time she had with her love, she had the immediate boomerang thought:

"And I will NEVER have another happy memory like that with HIM again."

And it would leave her weeping.

Can you see the persistent resistance (PR) in that? Can you see how self-sabotaging her ego was? That part of her mind, for whatever reason, was resisting her positive attitude!

When she came to see me, we jumped right on that phrase. I led her through a couple of rounds of tapping and within about 10 minutes we were able to tame her ego and release that resistance. This is the crux of the reframe that I intuited for her:

> *"If I had two 16th birthday parties, it would not be so special. Having only one makes it unique. Every unique memory is a gift and I would not want to have a second one anyway. That is why my precious memories are so precious. They are each unique, rare and mine alone."*

Memories are only "good" or "bad" because we judge and label them as such. Could you be willing, today, to accept and forgive them "as is?"

Grief Is . . . A Tower of Babble

You can hear people speaking, you have a sense they are trying to comfort you, but what they are saying makes little or no sense to you.

"Can you believe that he said that?" My client, Margaret, asked angrily.

Her tirade had lasted nearly ten minutes. We were tapping together swiftly as she talked. She told me story after story about all of the hurtful things people had said and done since her mother had passed.

The incident that seemed to agitate her the most at the moment was when her ex-husband, now remarried, had said to her, "It's good that your mother is not suffering anymore."

Margaret was incensed that he, the man who had caused her so much personal emotional suffering; he, the man who had been absent the last few years when she had to deal with all of the doctors, surgeries and decisions; *how could HE* the man who "wouldn't know nurturing if it bit him in the butt" (her words not mine) say such a thing? What she was really telling me was that she was hurting. She believed he was responsible for a portion of her pain and she was revoking his right to have any opinions.

"Margaret" I began softly. "I am so sorry that your friends and family have left you feeling so hurt and misunderstood." She nodded in agreement.

"So… how would you like to proceed this morning? Are you ready to try and release some of the hurt and anger?"

Her clenched jaw made her lips pucker slightly. She inhaled and exhaled loudly through her nose. She was looking at the floor and I sensed she was contemplating the idea. Maybe she didn't want to let it go?

"I guess…" she started and then stopped to say, "I just don't understand how the people that I have loved so much, and that I thought loved me, could be so thoughtless and insensitive."

"Yeah, I get that." I said tenderly. "How about if we start by just tapping on that feeling?" I tilted my head and waited for her to respond. She nodded yes and instinctively lifted up her hands to begin tapping.

We tapped for several minutes. Many times tears came and fell as we acknowledged how much she was hurting, how alone she felt, and then how sad she was that so many people had seemingly let her down.

Then we tapped on what she wished they would have done or said instead. When she was less angry about her inconsiderate friends, we tapped for her heartache over her mother's passing and how the pain sometimes seemed unbearable.

Within minutes, her tone began to soften. Her once pursed lips relaxed into a soft smile. She was obviously feeling much better.

Grief has a way of turning us inside out. The very people that we want closest to us are the ones who we may push away. We may be yearning inside for them to sit or stand quietly with us in our darkest hour. And yet, with our tender hearts reacting to their every word defensively, we inadvertently repel them.

In the darkness, amid the phantom memories and physical pain and sheer exhaustion, we may not realize that we don't even know what it is that we want to hear. We just know that nothing seems right. Nothing makes it feel better.

You may find yourself wondering, "What is wrong with everyone? Can't they see what I need? Do they hear themselves? I thought they knew me and now, it's like they don't get me at all.

When your heart is aching, anything that anybody says that does not affirm your pain the way that you need it to, can trigger your little EGO voices and stir up your defenses.

You may have already heard some of these so-called encouraging words:

"Things will get better, hang in there."

"Your stuff is replaceable; at least you have your health."
"You will find a better job."

Or, in the case of a lost loved one:

"They are in a much better place now."

"They had done all they could do in this lifetime."

"God must have a bigger mission for them in heaven."

"They are not suffering anymore."

When you hear such things, your ego may be telling you:

"What do you mean <u>a better place</u>? Are you saying that being here with me is a bad thing?"

Or: *"Right now, <u>I don't care</u> what God wants or what their mission was...I just want them back."*

111

Or more to the point: *"Don't tell me
what I should feel or think or do!"*

When people do say such things, it is
difficult - if not nearly impossible - to
remember that they are just trying to comfort
you. You are free to feel attacked or offended.
You are free to close off, isolate and suffer in
silence. Or, you can observe what others say
and look for the well-wish meaning behind it
and let it go.

Let's face it, people will always show you
who they are by what they say. They tell you
what they believe, what they fear, what they
would do in any given situation. Generally
speaking, what other people say has little, if
anything, to do with you or your needs. When
we are feeling strong and the lights are on in
our heart, we are generally more apt to just
brush it off and let them off the hook. When
we are in pain, we may be tempted to shoot
them instead. (Just kidding!)

Try and remember that they are doing the
best they can to guess how to comfort you.
Would it really be best if everyone just left you
alone?

There may come a time when someone
says something that you really do need to
address. If you can gently reflect back to them
what you heard them say in a way that lets

them hear it from your point of view, maybe you can feel less closed.

For example, "Mary-Beth, I hear you saying that my loved one is in a better place. While part of me could agree with that and I'm happy knowing they are no longer in pain or struggling in this life, can you imagine that at least in this moment, I still ache for them and do not find comfort in hearing that they are in a better place? I am not ready for that counsel right now, thank you."

I once spoke at a breast cancer survivors group. (I called them the "Happy Booby Club!") The women were each in the various stages of treatment and recovery. After sharing a bit about what I do and some of my favorite client success stories, I offered to tap with them. We tapped on the first couple of aspects of grief and then I invited them to share some pressing pain or challenges that we could work on together.

One young woman had been sitting with her arms folded tightly across her belly throughout the evening. I sensed that she was in tremendous emotional and physical pain. I invited her to share. Her tone was harsh and she seemed impatient and unimpressed with the whole program. She briefly told us how long she had been in treatment and a little about her journey with cancer thus far and with anger and impatience turned to me and said: "You know, all of your stories are sweet and you seem like a nice lady, but you really have no idea what we are going through."

I immediately softened my tone and wholeheartedly agreed. "You are absolutely right. I will, hopefully, never fully understand what you brave women are going through. That isn't really why I am here, though. I am here tonight to offer my help and support in reducing your suffering. Can you tell me, if you want to, what you are struggling with the most right now?"

She lifted her shoulders and dropped them in a big shrug and then with angst replied, "I just want to know what I am supposed to say to all of the insensitive people out there."

She stopped short of crying and I gave her time to see if she wanted to say more.

"Can you give me a for-instance?"

"Oh yeahhhh-" she said with emphasis and anger. "I was finally feeling well enough to go to the grocery store last week and this lady passed me in the aisle and said, what happened to your hair?! Can you believe that?"

Every woman in the room cringed. I put my hand to my heart as I felt her spirit crying. I said a quick prayer and then it came to me…

"First, let me say that I am so sorry that you experienced that." I looked deep into her eyes. I could not have felt more empathy for this woman at that moment.

"How about this?" I said with my very best sarcastic grin. "Well, thank you ma'am for noticing. DR. CHEMOTHERAPY has been doing my hair, what is your excuse?"

With that, the auditorium filled with laughter. Most importantly to me, the young woman's mouth fell open and, with eyebrows raised in mock shock, she covered her mouth with her hand…and she laughed.

This is a perfect example of grief as the tower of babble. The woman in the store was just running off at the mouth. She was babbling, thoughtlessly and unnecessarily. She was oblivious to the wound she had left on the heart of our young breast cancer survivor.

The scripture story of the tower of Babel tells us that at one point everyone in the world spoke the same language. The people decided to build a tower to show how supreme they were. In fact, the original Hebrew word Babel meant "gateway to God."

God spoke to them and instructed them to stop. They chose not to listen. Acting out of ego pride they decided they didn't need to listen to God. So, God decided that a fair consequence would be for him to make it so they couldn't understand each other. If they wouldn't listen to His words, He would confound theirs.

Can you imagine what it was like? Thousands of people were working to build that incredibly complicated structure. God delivers a message and they ignore it. So the next day two workers are sitting side by side adding mud to the bricks. One guy turns to the other and asks for more mud. The other guy doesn't move, he just stares at him. What? What does he want? What is he saying?

I can just see the two guys looking each other over, each repeating their requests over and over, each time speaking a little more slowly. Then they begin to over-enunciate as if that will help the other guy understand. Then, getting impatient and annoyed, they start adding a tone of condescension. The voices start getting louder and louder. And, of course, they would both be thinking *the other guy was the idiot*.

How long do you think it took before they were all so fed up with one another that they started walking off the job?

And then they would seek out someone, anyone that they could understand. They wanted someone who could speak their language. Sound familiar?

The work on the tower ceased. The people divided themselves into groups and moved away from the tower. After that, the Hebrew word Babel meant confusion.

I experienced similar confusion when my client, Sherry, lost her young husband and she quickly spiraled into depression. We had done some amazing work with tapping prior to her husband's death, however, after his death she refused to let me help her. I was forced to sit by helplessly and watch as her attitude and her behaviors pushed everyone away.

She showed up unexpectedly shortly after my son, Devin, died. Those few weeks after his death are a bit of a blur to me, but I vividly remember my last conversation with Sherry. She said, "You don't know what it's like to bury the man you were married to and shared a bed with."

I was speechless. I had no intention of competing with Sherry. It never crossed my mind to compare my situation to hers. I am not sure what response she was hoping for from me that day. From that moment, she chose to drift away. We became strangers, speaking very different languages. Sadly, I haven't heard from her since.

I have no hard feelings toward Sherry. I am not sure what I was supposed to say in response to her comment. The eternal optimist in me believes that she didn't intend to be mean. She was in pain and struck out at me from her ego.

I'll confess that - even knowing all of these skills - I still make some of the same mistakes. After my brother died from a heart attack in December of 2009, several of us were milling around the funeral home waiting for the visitation service to begin. I was overcome with love and compassion for my sister-in-law. I desperately wanted to reach out and comfort her. I wanted to express my gratitude for what a loving wife she had been.

I told her, "Thank you for loving my brother." As I said it, my mind flashed to a personal memory of being his little sister and being picked on. So, I added jokingly with a smile, "I know it wasn't always easy."

As soon as I said it, I felt her spirit close. It seemed all she heard was that I was disparaging her husband. I fumbled for the words to repair the hurt, but in that instant she walked away into the crowd before I could mend my mistake.

I failed to communicate the love and compassion that I was feeling in my heart because my mind (yup, my little ego voice) fractured my focus and interjected a selfish comment. DRAT! Yes, I am still learning.

Grief can be a tower of babble when it seems there is no one there to translate between the tortured mind of the grieving person and the eager, but inexperienced, heart of a loving friend or family member.

Words can become the red carpet or the wrecking ball in their power to open or close the person's spirit.

It is impossible to guess what will make the grieving person uncomfortable. It may be best to begin by asking for permission to talk now or, more specifically, to share your memories of the deceased.

If they welcome the opportunity to share your memories, remember to take a breath and pause often allowing them the space to converse with you.

Personally, I don't think there is anything more stressful than having someone talk at me, especially when they go on and on for more than ten minutes at a time.

It takes energy to talk when you're grieving. The emotion of grief is one of the lowest vibrations on the energy scale. The grieving person may feel that they simply do not have the energy to carry on a conversation, let alone listen intently.

Over time, the energy does come back and it may be helpful to have some ideas on how to initiate a conversation with your grieving love one. Here are a few of my suggestions:

"What I remember about (name)."

"I remember one time when (name)."

"I didn't really know (name). I feel like I have missed out on someone wonderful. If you are comfortable sharing about her/him, I would love to hear…"

"I cannot imagine how you are feeling right now. I am happy just to listen to you talk about it if you like."

"I imagine that if I were you right now I would be filled with thoughts and

emotions. Do you want to share with me what is going on inside of you?"

During special events, weddings, holidays it might be good to simply say:

"I am remembering (name). He/She is so missed. Would you like to talk about him/her?" Or "I would love to hear about him/her."

If you are afraid you will make the mistaking of babbling, simply think through what you might be inclined to say and then translate that for a hurting heart.

Here are a few examples to get you started.

THE EGO BABEL: "You look so tired." (Or you look so sad, or terrible, whatever your negative assessment might be.)

Pointing out that the person is not looking their best is both hurtful and depleting. Saying things like this will only make the person want to isolate more. (I know, we mean well!)

THE HEART TRANSLATION: "I am so happy to see you."

How can you go wrong with this comment? If the person struggled with the decision to show up, they are validated for having done so. You have offered them a welcome without any pressure or implied expectations. Accepting and loving them right where they are in the moment is truly the most healing gift you can give them.

THE EGO BABEL: "I know this must be so hard for you; when my (whatever happened or whoever) died..."

Telling someone how hard it is to grieve is a projection. You are imposing your perspective onto them and you may be wrong. These statements will certainly create a closed spirit.

If you are inclined to open the conversation by talking about your own experience, consider that talking about you or your past pain may also make them feel obligated to console, support or comfort you.

THE HEART TRANSLATION: "You may know that I have lost a child, too. I think every love lost is incomparable. I have no idea how you are feeling, but I'm a really great listener. If you need someone to talk to, I am here for you."

By first acknowledging that you are not trying to compete or compare their loss and pain with you or yours, you remove the emotional wall. You may even see a physical shift in their body language from cautious and quiet to relaxed and talkative.

Here are a few dangerous EGO BABEL words and phrases to avoid:
- You…
- You should…
- You shouldn't…
- Be (as in: be grateful that…)
- Isn't it…
- It's a good thing…
- I…
- When I…

Whenever you are tempted to offer advice or solutions, don't. It will probably be received as a criticism.

I often joke with my clients by saying, "Do not SHOULD on yourself today." The same goes for when you are trying to communicate with others. Keep your rules to yourself. (grin)

What a gift you will be to your friends, family and loved ones as you learn to truly offer unconditional love in times of tremendous life challenges.

Listen with your heart. Speak cautiously and consciously. With love as your translator, you will bring down the tower of babble every time.

Jan Luther

Grief Is . . . An Inconsiderate Guest

*It shows up uninvited
at the most inopportune times
and always overstays its welcome.*

Three days after his wife died from Alzheimer's disease, David returned to work. He told his boss that he needed to stay busy; being home alone was too much to bear.

Throughout the day he was greeted by one well-meaning soul after another offering him condolences. However, with each handshake and pat on the back, David felt closer and closer to tears. Speechless, he would simply look his colleague in the eye, nod and then hurry back to his office to close the door and cry.

Throughout the day David wrestled with his EGO mind. He would be working on a project when his thinking would fracture, wander off without permission and begin reminiscing.

There was a lot to remember from the past ten years. Each memory played out in vivid detail on the movie screen of his mind. He revisited the day his wife was given the dreadful diagnosis. He rehearsed the hundreds of conversations they had shared about feeling embarrassed, afraid and ashamed by what was happening to her body; she hated that she was losing control.

He didn't remember exactly when it happened, but somewhere on their journey he got mad at the disease and he began to fight for her life.

He had devoted hours and hours to researching Alzheimer's. He acted upon every promising piece of information. He hired the best holistic practitioners, adjusted what they were eating, brought in a home care provider and, on several occasions, they traveled out of town for her to receive treatments.

At one point, when it was no longer safe for her to drive, David rearranged his schedule, rising every morning at 4:00 a.m. and working a few hours so that he could be available at 9:00 a.m. to drive her over to pick up their grandson and drop him off at his school. It meant so much to her.

And then there were the memories of her last few hours on earth. His mind seemed to be addicted to watching those movies the most. Over and over it would replay the conversations with the hospice nurse, with the family and friends, with his pastor. Time and again, David would realize he was crying, shake his head and force his mind to focus on the work in front of him.

Maybe he would be able to stay on task a few minutes or, if he was lucky, an hour. But, inevitably his mind would hijack his attention again and again.

When it seemed that the past memories were not creating enough distress, his mind would jump into worrying about his future. Would he ever be able to face the empty house without crying? What about their grandson? How would he cope with the holidays without her?

By 2:00 that afternoon, David was exhausted. He certainly was not having success at staying on task. Frustrated with his lack of productivity, he went to his supervisor and, with apologies, excused himself for the day.

It would be months before David would be able to make his mind stay at work with him for a full eight-hour day. Yes, his body was there all day, but his heart and mind were on a constant journey through his grief.

No doubt David would tell you that grief was an inconsiderate guest at work. He was experiencing first-hand how grief will 'inner-fear' with every aspect of our lives.

In November, 2002, *The Wall Street Journal* published an article written by Jeffrey Zaslow: *New Index Aims to Calculate the Annual Cost of Despair*.

In the article he reported on a study, called the **Grief Index**, compiled by The Grief

Recovery Institute which estimated that workplace grief costs U.S. businesses over $75 billion a year in lost productivity, increased errors and accidents.

You can view the entire article at:

http://www.griefrecoverymethod.com/press/new-index-aims-to-calculate-the-annual-cost-of-despair/

I spoke with Russell Friedman, executive director of The Grief Recovery Institute and primary author of the **Grief Index**. Russell had read the story of what happened to David in the aftermath of his wife's death and said that David's experience was parallel to many of the 25,000 grieving people he and his associates have talked with over two decades of teaching the Grief Recovery Method. (You can check out their web site at www.griefrecoverymethod.com.)

Friedman said, "Inability to concentrate," both in the short and long-term, which reflects David's saga to a tee, is the primary cause of grief-related non function in the workplace.

Friedman also said, "When your heart is broken, your head doesn't work right, and when your heart is broken, your spirit cannot soar. The heart dominates your life when you are beset by a grief producing event, and you must take direct actions to deal with the grief and unresolved grief before you can really function effectively again."

The statistics published in the Grief Index, highlighting the $75 Billion impact of grief in the workplace are staggering:

- Death of a Loved One Cost: $37.6 billion
- Divorce/Marital Woes Cost: $11 billion
- Family Crisis Cost: $9 billion
- Death of an Acquaintance Cost: $7 billion
- Money Trouble at Home Cost: $4.6 billion
- Pet Loss Cost: $2.4 billion

Obviously, grief is a nuisance at work. What about the other sixteen hours a day?

Imagine that it's a beautiful day. You are driving along in your car, windows down and the cool air twirling your hair when a song comes on the radio that triggers your grief. How did that happen? One minute you are fine and the next you're on the verge of tears. Can you breathe? Should you pull over or keep driving? What will you do?

Grief showed up unexpectedly and certainly uninvited.

Or perhaps you hear a story of someone who has the good fortune to get the job, buy the house or find the love of their life and it reminds you that you once had that. The little ego voice diverts all of your attention away from the present moment and, like the ghost of Christmas past, begins to escort you through memory after memory of "before." You cannot help but feel sad. Grief has arrived and it looks like it is planning to stay a while.

Or maybe you're walking into church and someone approaches you to offer you their love and support. Instead of feeling uplifted, you suddenly want to cry. As the air goes out of your lungs, and the lump swells up in your throat threatening to choke you, you find yourself stunned and confused. Why do kind words and condolences usher in grief?

As I mentioned in an earlier chapter, I believe that when we receive shocking and dreadful news, our spirit closes. When our spirit is closed, the energy stops flowing and often we become a bit numb. This response can protect us from being overwhelmed by our emotions; for a while. But, eventually we all have to "check back in."

Sincere expressions of love and compassion are a very sacred key to opening the door to a wounded heart. Once that door is open and the resistance is down, the energy and emotions cannot help but gush out. Suddenly, the numbness is gone and you feel everything with tremendous intensity. It can be very disconcerting. Add to that the inner battle between the little ego voice and the voice of your higher self or Soul.

Ego might say, "Let it out! You deserve to cry! You want everyone to know how much you are hurting. Show them how much it hurts!" The ego certainly wants everyone to know how badly you feel. When it is miserable, the ego wants lots of company!

And then your Soul may pipe up and say, "Don't cry! Everyone will get uncomfortable and be upset. You don't want to ruin everyone's day! There is nothing they can do or say that will make it better anyway! And if you do carry on and upset everyone, then you will feel embarrassed and guilty afterward."

Which voice will you listen to? What should you do? Is there anything that you *can* do?

The first response when grief rushes in on us is often fear. But, fear of what, I would ask you? You have already suffered the trauma or loss. Where is this fear coming from?

After interviewing dozens of my clients, we have discovered two possible answers. Fear may arise because of the constricted breathing; or fear may be a reaction to negative thoughts in the moment.

When prompted to sift out the thought that precedes or accompanies the fear feeling, my clients always offer some version of "I am afraid I will cry." Once we have that nugget, I ask them what fear is behind that. They might say "I would be embarrassed to cry in public" or occasionally they will say "I am afraid if I start crying, I won't be able to stop."

Notice that both fears are about losing control.

Have you ever experienced those thoughts or feelings? Can you find a specific memory when grief showed up unexpectedly and you panicked?

Let's tap for that fear.

"Even though I have this fear that if I start crying I will not be able to stop, I deeply and completely love and appreciate that I do not want to lose control.

Even though I have this idea that if I start crying I will not be able to stop, I deeply and completely honor this idea; even if I have never heard of someone crying uncontrollably forever without eventually stopping.

Even though I think I would be sooo embarrassed if I started to cry in front of (who) someone, I deeply and completely accept that crying is an expression of how I am feeling.

My feelings are clearly reasonable under the circumstances. Maybe I am afraid of my own opinions about people who cry. . .

How do I feel about my feelings?
How do I feel about myself or others if we cry?
Am I embarrassed by what I feel...or how deeply I feel?
Do I really believe I will cry uncontrollably, forever?
Has that ever happened to me in the past?
I would like to release this fear, now."

Another way that you can control your emotions is by using what I have affectionately named **"The Luther Grief Breathing Method."**

Following the analogy I mentioned in chapter one - the similarities between birthing and deathing a child - I realized that expectant mothers are taught specific breathing techniques to help them relax and focus during their painful contractions. I decided that I would like to adapt this idea and find a way to use breathing to allay an oncoming crying attack. To my amazement, I found a way that works!!

First we need to look at the physiology of a grief attack.

Remember that there is always a trigger; a scent, sound or memory quickly followed by the physical reaction. The reaction is a sort of 'contraction' of our lungs. It is as if someone has knocked the air out of you. The lungs deflate and the diaphragm collapses. When your breathing is constricted, the body, depleted of oxygen begins to send panic signals to the brain. Unfortunately, the panic only adds to the fear and now the brain goes into fight, flight and freeze mode.

If you do nothing, the cycle of gasping for air and the feelings of terror escalate until you either, run away, explode in tears or yelling, or you melt into a crying heap. Who wants that, right?

So if you are in a situation where you feel a grief attack coming on and you do not want to give in to the tears, try The Luther Grief Breathing Method.

There are three components to this method:

1. Place both hands on the bottom of your ribs and immediately begin tapping.

2. Roll your shoulders forward slightly, EXHALE hard and BEAR DOWN, compressing your chest and pushing your belly OUT. Yes, force the abdomen to pooch out below your naval.

3. Then, to the count of five, inhale through your nose, drawing the air up from your abdomen, sucking in your gut and puffing your chest out while rolling your shoulders back.

To watch a video describing this breathing method, please use the link below. You can also use your smartphone to scan the QR Code below.

http://griefismourningsickness.com/luther-grief-breathing-method/

This method is most effective when you catch the grief attack as soon as it starts. The moment you feel your diaphragm begin to contract - or when you notice the pressure on your chest - roll your shoulders forward; resist the contracting diaphragm by bearing down and pushing your belly out. Then, to the count of five, inhale slowly and deeply through your nose, over-exaggerating the act of filling your lungs.

Notice that we are doing several things at once. We are focusing on breathing consciously through the nose which helps to slow down the mental chatter, quieting the mind and short-circuiting the fear response.

By pooching and pushing out the belly we are resisting the contraction of the diaphragm and forcing the muscles to relax. We are then taking in an abundance of oxygen, feeding the muscles, tissues and brain and allaying the fear feelings. And, of course, by adding tapping we stop the disruption of the energy system. When we do these three simple steps, our mind is drawn back to the present moment. More relaxed and feeling safe, you may naturally yawn or sigh automatically.

With a little practice you will find that this method will instantly stop your tears. The feeling of being overtaken by grief gently melts away. Then you are free to choose what, if anything, to say or do next. Empowering, right?!

Now, you may be thinking, "Isn't short circuiting these emotions unhealthy? If I do this won't I just be detaching from the feelings or avoiding the healing process?"

I would submit to you that it is not. I don't intend for you to use this method every time you are feeling grief. It is ideally for times when you are in public or in a situation where "losing it" will not be helpful; or you may choose to use this if there is ever a time when you have been crying for a time and you want to stop.

We would certainly never hope to entertain grief. As with any guest, we can decide to take charge of our home and space! What would you do with an unwanted house guest?

You would most likely set boundaries and rules for them. You would define how long they could stay, where they should sleep, what and where they might eat, how much attention they can expect from you, etc. I suggest you take the same approach with your grieving process.

Why not begin by creating a space where you can be alone to think the thoughts and feel the feelings that constitute grief work. At the cemetery, in your bedroom, some particularly quiet space in your home or in nature.

Let's face it, we are physical beings. We live through our senses. Having someone suddenly disappear from our lives is one of the most traumatic elements of losing them. Creating a physical space and then adding keepsakes can be incredibly comforting. Remember, though, that their effects will have an effect on you.

Be careful not to sabotage your progress by choosing things that actually trigger more pain or self-pity. Can you select something of theirs that always makes you smile?

Grieving is a natural process that will demand your time and attention sooner or later. If you avoid the work, grief will inevitably show up in your life; somewhere, sometime, maybe when you least expect it.

Why not decide today that you are open to entertaining grief? Greet it on your own terms. Welcome the opportunity to manage the relationship consciously so that, in due time, you can send it on its way and get back to your life!

Jan Luther

Grief Is . . . Oil in the Salad Dressing of Life

Trauma, loss and change have a way of bringing even the busiest of lives to a complete halt. As the shaking and quaking of your daily routine stops, you may find that, like oil in salad dressing, past grievances and pains float to the top of your attention waiting to be skimmed out of your life.

I marched past the woman in the parking deck dragging my little rolling suitcase behind me. The whirling of its wheels thumped and hummed; a happy sound matching my mood.

My swift pace quickly set me on the heels of a well-dressed middle-aged woman. Her beautiful black and silver hair was in a tight bun. Long red fingernails graced her hands as she smoothed the front of her coat. As I rapidly maneuvered my way around her, I could see a man a few yards ahead of her pushing a huge luggage cart. The cart was piled four feet high.

Three large trunks formed the foundation. On top of the trunks, several large suitcases in blue and black and even a polka-dot rolling bag. The pile was topped with two carry-on bags, one of which was a huge neon yellow purse with shoulder straps and it was bouncing up and down in rhythm with his steps.

"I am going to Vegas baby! Outa my way!" I thought to myself as I passed the man and threw him a smile.

I could hear the engine of the shuttle bus revving up, slowing and stopping several times as it zigzagged its way through the airport parking lot.

I walked right up to the pick-up stand, third in line, just as the bus brakes squealed and creaked and then released their puff of air, stopping the bus in front of us. Patiently, methodically, we each stepped forward and took the two steps up and onto the bus. We each eyed the available seats as we waited our turn to swing our suitcases waist high onto the luggage rack.

I took my seat by the far window. The couple behind me found their seats and everyone began minding their own business. Within seconds we were each in our own world; looking at our tickets, cell phones or the black rubber mats that covered the bus floor.

And then, there they were; the man, the woman and the mountain of luggage. It was as if we all had the same thought at the same time. We exchanged impatient half smiles as our visions of a quick trip to our departure gates went up in smoke.

Sure enough, the conscientious bus driver turned off the engine, skipped off the bus and graciously began to assist the travelers with their heap of luggage.

No one was going anywhere for a while.

Life is like that sometimes. You are in the flow, dreaming your dreams, planning your plans and errrch, something happens that brings your life to a halt.

And nothing halts life like grief.

Janice's life had come to a halt. In the midst of handling all of the details for her mother's funeral, her nearly forgotten old boyfriend appeared.

"Why is he showing up NOW?" She asked me.

She told me the whole disheartening story of how several years earlier, this man - whom she would have called the 'love of her life' - broke up with her and left town. They had never spoken since the big fight.

Yet, there he was at her mother's funeral, expressing sympathy and being so kind and gentle with her. And she "simply could not bring herself to forgive him at a time like this."

Janice had been caught off guard. She hadn't expected to see him – ever - let alone now at this very vulnerable time.

It could be an old family friend or neighbor, an old teacher or a black-sheep relative. It happens all the time. When grief comes to visit, it may bring with it the very people you have been trying to avoid.

It didn't take much coaxing to convince Janice to tap on the memory of her ex-boyfriend. We began by clearing the shock and confusion that accompanied the fight.

Then we addressed her feelings of betrayal at the way he disappeared. We found half a dozen memories - as vivid as if they had happened yesterday - and melted them away, one by one.

Within minutes she was feeling better and her once closed spirit began to soften. As we tapped she could see that some great things had occurred after he left town; things that could not have happened if he had stayed.

Then she realized that maybe he was just as hurt and scared as she was about how their relationship had ended; and, yet, he had found the courage to show up.

Would she have resented him more if he didn't show?

Soon, she was able to connect with the memories of how much her ex-boyfriend had loved her mother. As the loving memories flowed she became more and more peaceful and compassionate.

Before we closed the session I circled back and we tapped on several aspects of her missing her wonderful loving mother. What an amazing woman she was; how much she was like her. Once her spirit was open it was easy for Janice to decide what she would do.

A few weeks later, Janice reported joyfully that she was able to reach out to her ex-boyfriend and express sincere appreciation for his making the effort to show his respects to her mother. She told me she was able to hug him as they parted without any hint of old hurt or discomfort.

Another client, Leonard, was struggling with grief. He was feeling more and more depressed and hopeless after his sister died. As soon as he came to see me we began working through the five aspects of grief. Within hours, he was breathing easier and feeling relief. While we were working, he kept having old memories pop-up.

He remembered a time in the service when he was passed over for advancement. He was still angry and resentful toward that superior officer.

He remembered a fight with his father when he was only a teenager.

He remembered when there had been a misunderstanding with his teacher in grade school and he could not get the principal, his mother or his father to believe him.

When each of these hurtful memories would show up I would ask Leonard if we could tap on them. Over and over he resisted, saying he "didn't really want to talk about his those things; that was not why he was seeing me."

I absolutely understood why he was resisting. At first glance it would seem that these are "unrelated stories." What I have discovered, however, is that when we are given the opportunity to heal our grief, our subconscious mind will gladly clean out our emotional closets.

Leonard had never devoted time or energy to healing all of the disappointments and anger all those years. He had no idea that these incidents were the proverbial "emotional baggage" that he had been carrying. The weight of the loss of his sister brought him to his knees.

Thankfully, he accepted my offer to address all of the other stories and he was more and more relieved and delighted at the close of each hour. As I escorted him to his car after one particular visit he gave me a hearty hug and said, and I quote, "I swear that when I leave your office I can see better. The colors (of the trees) are crisp and vibrant. I feel better than I have in years."

One of the many gifts of grief is that it has a way of bringing up our unfinished business- so we can finish it!

Almost every client I work with discovers that the primary reason they come to see me may not be what we end up working on. The initial challenge is always connected to other stories, beliefs and incidents from the past. The stories that rise up for healing may or may not seem to make any logical sense.

That is another amusing attribute of the ego; it tends to connect things that don't seem to be connected.

Sometimes I think that is my greatest gift to my clients - being able to show them the threads that the ego has woven between the many seemingly unrelated stories and clip them.

I often use the analogy for my clients that we each walk through life with a silver tray in one hand. Every life experience leaves something on the tray. Over time, broken dreams, betrayals, disappointments and grief begin to weigh on the tray and the burden becomes more than we can carry.

And then one day something happens and it is "the last straw." The weight of it all becomes too much to carry. The tray begins to tilt and threatens to spill all over the ground. You may squat, lunge and bobble trying to balance it all, but if you don't find a way to unload some of the pain from your past, eventually the tray topples over and you are left picking up the pieces.

Grief can bring up multitudes of opportunities for healing. By being open to addressing your unfinished business whenever it shows up, you can quickly and easily tame the ego.

A key benefit of taming the ego is creating a quiet mind. When the mind is quiet, you can hear the whispers of inspiration that come through your heart and soul. In the stillness, wisdom rises up with fresh hope, courage and clear direction. Operating from this deep, calm and more spiritually alert part of your being, miracles abound.

Grief can be a wonderful catalyst for bringing out the best in you.

Jan Luther

Grief Is . . . A Marathon

Grief is not a sprint; it is a marathon over innumerable hurdles of firsts.

I could hear the desperation in Rhonda's voice. "When will I start feeling better?"

"Am I grieving right?" Barbara begged.

"Will I ever feel like my old self again?" Kendal wondered out loud.

These are just a few of the hundreds of unanswerable questions that I have been asked over the years about grief. I never pretend to have answers to these questions.

This much I know for sure: if you do nothing, you get nothing.

Over and over I have heard well-meaning people counsel a grieving person to "just give it time." I disagree.

Without hesitation, I can tell you that every client who works with me using tapping finds major relief in a <u>matter of hours</u>, not months. Most will tell you that their only regret is that they did not know about me, or tapping, sooner.

I have worked with clients who book sessions with me within days of their trauma, loss or change. Others book within weeks or months of their incident. Frequently, clients that I work with have been struggling with some level of grief for years.

In working with thousands of clients over the years, tapping has proven to be effective every time.

While time does little to heal your grief, I want to share with you some of the experiences you will want to anticipate as you are traveling the road through grief. The following are some of the many firsts that can trigger grief within the first year or two of losing a loved one.

Obviously, the first weeks are the most excruciating because everything you do, every thought you think, will be a "first time" without your loved one. Here is a list of firsts to be prepared for:

- The first time you see family and friends and everyone is grieving the loss.
- The first time you think about "their" favorites - song, food, color, or friend.
- The first time you touch their "stuff" after they are gone.
- The first time you look at pictures.
- Your own first private memories of them.
- The first time you have a moment of peace and you forget they are gone and you think about calling them...and it hits

you...and you begin to grieve all over again.

- The first thing in the morning when you awaken...and remember again.
- The first time you see, hear, or smell something that you know they would enjoy.
- The first time someone asks about them because they didn't know.
- The first time someone tells you something that you didn't already know about them.
- The first time you have to decide to think about it or not to think about it.
- The first birthday, anniversary, holidays.
- The first wedding, funeral, family reunion.
- The first time one of their friends accomplishes something or makes a pivotal life step and you think about what might have been....again... and again.
- The first time you *don't* cry yourself to sleep.
- The first time you actually smile.
- The first time you fully laugh, even if you are tempted to feel guilty about it.
- The first time you can tell the story and not fall apart.
- The first time you feel them or see them in a dream or imagine them with you.

- The first time you are strong enough to just listen to someone else who is grieving.
- The first time you have the opportunity to share the wisdom and experience you earned by passing through and getting beyond grief.

It is my hope that by knowing what to expect when you are grieving you will be better prepared to cope.

I would encourage you to consider finding a qualified Tapping Practitioner to assist and support you through these pivotal points of grief.

Jan Luther

Grief Is . . . A Day-to-Day Experience.

Every day brings some degree of change. Virtually every change means a loss of some kind. Depending upon the degree of attachment to the person, place or situation that was lost, there is an equal degree of trauma and readjustment to the new normal. Life is full of grief.

When you think of grief, do you automatically think "someone died?" After years of working with clients on everything from eating disorders to addictions and repeating unhealthy relationship patterns, I can assure you that grief is about much more than the death of a loved one.

When Benjamin celebrated his first birthday, he was one happy baby! A few months later, his mother decided it was time to wean him off of his pacifier. Benjamin didn't understand. He may have felt that not getting what he wanted was like taking away love. He adjusted pretty well during the day but at night he cried and cried. No one died, but Benjamin was grieving.

Jackie clung to her mother's skirt at the kindergarten room door. She didn't want to be a "big girl" if it meant she had to leave her mommy. She wet her bed that night and several nights after. No one died, but Jackie was grieving.

Danny was 15 when his first love Becky moved to another city with her family. He didn't feel like eating. He was moody and lost interest in school, sports and socializing for several months. No one died, but Danny was grieving.

After Rhonda got married, she and her husband built a fabulous real estate business. Soon they had two children and they were enjoying a life of ease and fun. When the economy bottomed out, real estate sales dried up. Rhonda had to take a second job. The marriage was strained. The family had to quickly make cutbacks, including selling the teenager's car, cancelling the family vacation, and dropping some of their favorite memberships. No one died, but the family was grieving.

I could tell you hundreds of stories of people who have been stuck in their past, wishing something had played out differently. These people may or may not have lost anyone, but the trauma, loss or change of an everyday experience absolutely left them grieving.

Let me give you a few more examples:

Paula was just out running an errand one day when she had a really bad car accident. When she finally returned home from the hospital she was afraid to go to sleep. She had nightmares every night and, worse yet, she refused to drive for weeks. Paula was traumatized; she had lost her sense of safety.

The accident changed how she felt about herself, driving and life. No one died, but Paula was grieving.

After one tapping session with me the mental movies stopped. She reported that she slept for the first time since her accident. The anxiety diminished and, after a couple more sessions, she was able to enjoy driving again.

Richard was only 38 when he had a heart attack. After months of recovery he reported to me that he felt angry and afraid every day. He had lost his confidence. Obviously, the experience was traumatic. He had also lost confidence in his body. We did a lot of work around feeling like his body had let him down and even attacked him. Everything changed for Richard and his family the day he was hospitalized. No one died, but everyone was grieving.

Jennifer was diagnosed with breast cancer. Several months after her treatment, her doctor told her that she was now experiencing PTSD (Post Traumatic Stress Disorder). She called for a series of tapping sessions to treat the PTSD. We worked for a session or two on the trauma of having a life-altering diagnosis. The trauma of that day in the doctor's office brought tremendous loss and change to life as she had known it. No one had died, but Jennifer was grieving.

Grief is present when we move and lose our community of friends (including being excommunicated or shut out of a church or social group).

Grief is present when we get a divorce.

Grief is present when we lose a limb, when we enter a new season in life, and even when we fail to accomplish a dream.

Grief really is a day-to-day experience.

There comes a point in each person's life when they must decide:

Am I going to let my disappointment and my grief dictate how I feel about life or am I going to face these feelings and get back in the game?

If you cannot imagine feeling like yourself again, if you cannot imagine having happy and joyful moments again, hold on - you can and you will!

Like my sweet daughter in the midst of her labor wondering if the pain would ever end or if the baby would ever be delivered - these feelings, too, shall pass.

DON'T GIVE UP!

I tell my story and I coach others through negative experiences like trauma, loss and change because I have learned, first-hand, that you can feel joy again.

Defining grief helps take the power back.

Having tools and systematic healing programs helps to quicken the recovery. Learn them. Apply them. Become your own practitioner!

Jan Luther

One of the primary tools in tapping is called the "movie technique." The client is asked to describe the distressing memory as if it was a movie and the practitioner notes all of the key elements or aspects of the story.

For example, if we are addressing the trauma of a car accident; the client will obviously remember the physical aspect of driving and the impact of the crash. What is less obvious is that their mind and body will have captured enormous amounts of information through all of their senses.

If I were facilitating a session with a client to release the trauma of a car accident I would start by asking them to direct their full attention to what I call the "space and time" of the incident.

Some common questions would be: Do you remember the date? What day of the week? What time of day? What was the weather like? What road or highway were you driving on? Where were you going?

Then we would collect all the visual memories: What did you see? Do you remember seeing the other car or the road hazard prior to the moment of impact? Did you see - and can you describe for me - the expressions on any co-passengers' faces? Do you remember what you were wearing?

Next might be auditory memories: What did you hear when you began to remember the accident? Do you remember tidbits of conversations or the sounds of voices, music or maybe even the sound of the tires on the road or the brakes screeching? I might also ask about what I call "dreadful words;" what, if anything, did the passengers, other driver or the police officer say? Did you overhear something upsetting at the scene, in the ambulance or at the hospital?

Can you recall the smell of gasoline, cologne, burnt rubber or the gun powder that came from the air bag activating?

I would then ask my client to remember and describe what they remember feeling physically at the moment of impact.

Just to clarify: Were you driving the car or were you a passenger? Do you remember holding onto the steering wheel? Did your hands grip the wheel and your body brace for impact? Do you remember the sensation of your body snapping forward and then backward?

Piece by piece, element by element, I interview them to help them remember and associate with every possible aspect.

One aspect I always ask about that has proven very powerful is the aspect of intuition or premonition. I like to ask the client if they had any sense of foreboding before the incident. Most, if not all, of my clients admit they experienced some little internal warning that they may have ignored.

Maybe they had a feeling that they should not go out that day. Or maybe they hesitated before getting behind the wheel. Maybe they simply had a fleeting thought that they should not drive that particular route.

If they did not heed any one of these intuitive warnings, they will probably be struggling with added layers of regret and guilt.

I would then begin tapping with them on whatever their self-condemning phrase might be such as, "It's all my fault. I knew I should have – or shouldn't have… whatever."

After clearing any such regrets I like to anchor and affirm that they now have undeniable confirmation that listening to inner wisdom is important. We would probably tap on any worry or fear of what others might think or say if they listen to their intuition as opposed to that which appears logical.

We would tap to decide which is more important to their safety; trusting their inner wisdom - even if they can't explain why they feel what they feel - or letting the fear of looking foolish to their friends put everyone in harm's way.

One of the delightful secondary benefits of addressing this aspect is that my clients begin to accept and even expect that they are guided and inspired by unforeseen spiritual support. They are never alone.

Once we have uncovered and tapped on the key aspects, I may even go one step farther and ask them to tell me about the next few minutes or hours after the incident. If there were far-reaching circumstances, we may even discuss what happened a few days, months or even years after the accident.

The process is very gentle and highly effective. Because we address each aspect with what one might call reverence, the client is able to calmly process all of the information that overloaded their circuits and kept the movie looping in their mind, thus keeping the energy and emotions disrupted.

Over the years I have discovered that since every incident is filled with aspects and every aspect is connected to other stories, we can uncover and dissolve a myriad of past traumas by working one highly stressful incident. By intentionally digging deeper into each tidbit, my clients experience a deep and permanent healing of the trauma.

Finding and clearing as many aspects as you can find in a story are absolutely essential to the effective application of tapping.

So, that begs the question: Are there specific and unique aspects beyond the six senses that consistently surface during the grieving process?

YES!

In fact, I have discovered that there are five. After years of testing this theory, I am confident that every practitioner, coach and grieving person will recognize that there are indeed predictable patterns and pathways that the mind travels through on the journey of grief.

When I first toyed with the idea of looking for aspects of grief, I turned to the longstanding authority on grief: Elisabeth Kübler-Ross in her book, *On Death and Dying*. In that book she teaches what she calls "The 5

<u>Stages</u> of Grief." These stages are known by the acronym DABDA:

1. Denial: This isn't really happening
2. Anger: This is not fair, why me, who is to blame?
3. Bargaining with God: I will do anything if You . . .
4. Depression: It doesn't matter, I am going to die anyway.
5. Acceptance: This is going to happen, I better prepare for it.

Over the years I had given her book to my clients, taught the five stages in workshops and even tried to apply the stages to many of my own grieving experiences.

What I discovered was that, while insightful, the *Five Stages* as Kübler-Ross outlined them often leave us wanting for a solution or a plan of action for addressing those stages.

So I began to explore how her 5 Stages of Grief might be complimented with The 5 Aspects of Grief and tapping. **Using these aspects we can actually do something about those five stages!**

It was easy to establish that Kübler-Ross' *first four stages* of grief are actually all forms of such resistance: Denial, Anger, Bargaining -

and yes, based on my experience, even Depression is a form of resistance.

Mentally and emotionally, if not verbally, the person is saying: "NO, NO, NO!"

The mind may ticker-tape a dozen different phrases, but at their foundation each phrase exemplifies a NO response:

"I don't want to do this!" (NO)
"This wasn't supposed to happen!" (NO)
"Why did this happen to me?" (NO)

Notice that these phrases do not argue or pretend that the event (the trauma, loss or change) has not happened; the phrases simply declare that the client does not want to accept the experience.

Now, just to clarify, I do know what true denial looks like. When my mother was dying, my father was clearly in denial. He went about his day-to-day business talking about "when Momma gets better." That, to me, is being in denial. He refused to accept the fact that she was dying. He was going to pretend it wasn't so because he simply was not ready to face the truth. I honored his need to keep hoping for her recovery. Certainly time would persuade him to see and respond differently and, of course, it did.

Personally, when I was standing in the morgue looking at my son's body, there was no part of me in denial. I didn't deny it was him. I didn't deny he was dead. There was no room for such pretenses. I was shocked, yes. I was filled with emotion and **resistance** *yes*, but it was never part of my process to deny that he was gone.

When my clients tell me about the moment they received their dreadful news, they rarely, if ever, share that they didn't actually believe it. Few, if any, tried to deny it. They do, however, always mention that they had a strong reaction of confusion, closing of the spirit and passionate resistance to the news. Such dramatic changes simply do not make sense to the logical mind in that moment. We call this shock.

Regardless of how long ago the incident was, a part of the client will be "frozen in time." In fact, I like to forewarn my new practitioners in training not to be surprised if their client's body re-experiences the shock symptoms during the session. Once we tap into the deep energy and emotion of that shock, it's not unusual to physically shake and shudder as we process and release all of those emotions that never had the chance to fully process prior to the session. Just keep tapping.

Our goal for addressing the first aspect of grief is to help the client gently "inch their way" toward digesting the information that was overwhelming and unbearable at the time.

Thus I aptly refer to the **first aspect of grief as "Getting your head around it" or, in some cases, "Getting over your verdicts and vows."**

We do this by reviewing the movie, gathering all of the aspects of the six senses and then zeroing in on the resistant thoughts they had at the moment they got the news. I am especially looking for any dramatic decisions that were made - verdicts and vows - afterward.

Some examples of teeter-totter phrases that might help the client reframe or begin to accept the story for the first aspect part one ("Getting your head around it") are:

"I can't believe this happened - Maybe I will be ready to believe this soon."

"This is not fair – Of course it is not fair, yet. Fairness has little to do with my ability to take this all in and begin my healing."

"I don't want to do this – Who in their right mind would wish for this? Not wanting to do it does not mean I am not capable of it when I am ready."

Notice that all we need to do is soften the resistance. I am trying to fully acknowledge the resistance and introduce a possibility now, or in the near future, that will allow the spirit to open and feel hope.

The same approach is taken with the second part of the first aspect ("Getting over your verdicts and vows"):

Do you remember sometime in the past when someone said or did something and you got ticked off and made some off-handed - or maybe even seriously thought out - declaration?

For example, when my sibling talked me into climbing on the tin roof of the shed in the summer time and then left me there all day...(I am giggling now but I sure wasn't then) I decided (the Verdict) that I would NEVER trust him again and that I would NEVER do that to our little brother (Vow). Silly example, but I imagine that you get the point.

The problem with these Verdicts and Vows is that we are now trapped by them; doomed to live by the limits they place on our hearts, minds and relationships.

Vowing to never trust my brother again may have meant that I would have no one to turn to when I needed serious marriage advice. It would certainly affect how open and loving we could be to one another.

So imagine the number of verdicts and vows that are made at the time of serious trauma, loss or change. How would we soften our commitment to them so that we might introduce the idea of choices?

Shall we toy with a couple of random examples?

"I will be brokenhearted forever...if I want to be. I may wish to change my mind about that later."

"I will never forgive – that is my right. I always have that choice. It is good to know that being forgiving is an option."

When I am trying to assist the client with such verdicts and vows, my goal is to simply introduce the awareness that they are choosing deliberately. This awareness can go a long way to keeping them feeling trapped and powerless over their pain. As long as we are conscious of our choices...we can change.

The next aspect was no surprise to me, having looped around this one for months. You see, my relationship with my son was pretty typical - we butted heads a lot. In fact, someone described mothering teenage boys as playing bumper cars. There was always a power struggle or a resistance to conforming to the family rules.

Aspect two is: "Regrets from the past!"

If you have ever sat with someone after the loss of a loved one or after a divorce or disaster, it doesn't take long for everyone to begin reminiscing.

Unfortunately, the first memories that seem to surface are often saturated with guilt or regret. I have come to wonder if it is maybe because our mind is always trying to match memories by emotion. With the onset of grief our energy drops and our mood is sad. Thus any incident from our past that is colored with sadness may be the first to surface.

As you read in Chapter Six, *An Inconsiderate Guest*, when David went back to work he was understandably sad. His mind was consumed by sad memories. The most pervasive was, of course, any memory that affirmed his despairing belief that he had failed to rescue his sweetheart from her disease. As he was plagued by this perception, his mind hashed and rehashed some of the darkest moments of her journey. He was obsessing on the sad moments that filled him with guilt and regret.

We address these regrets again by reviewing the mental movies. After gently releasing the first aspects that accompany the shock, the mind is calmer and we are more open to seeing a bigger picture or a new angle on the experience – which, of course, is a reframe of the memories.

When David told me of his regret that he felt ("he should have done more"), we tapped on those feelings; all the while recalling the ten thousand things he did that were above and beyond loving and supportive. Soon, he was able to choose to stop listening to the little ego voice that seemed to want to add insult to his injuries by convincing him that if he had done something different, she would still be with him.

Anyone that has experienced grief will tell you that it is an exhausting process. You'll find that this is, in part, because the mind is so twitchy. By that I mean that it is nearly impossible to keep one train of thought for very long. Like a jack rabbit, the mind will hop from thoughts of persistent resistance to thoughts of regrets; and then in a heartbeat bolt into the future, imagining pain and disappointments that were never experienced!

For example, one of the early thoughts that popped into my mind soon after my 22-year old son died was, "He will never meet his twin nieces." I understand that this is the mind's way of anticipating and preparing for a future *without* the person, place or things that has been lost. Oddly enough, however, these "Imagined Future Disappointments" that I consider the third aspect of grief are often of the "fairy tale" variety.

When Clara was working through her grief and the holidays were quickly approaching, she was inundated with "imagined future disappointments" about the family gatherings. Upon further inspection, the story she was imagining was unrealistic. She envisioned that Momma would cook all of their favorite dishes. The family would laugh and visit for hours. Then everyone would part with hugs and promises to get together every month for Sunday dinner or something.

So, do I need to tell you what I discovered when I explored her fairy tale wish?

The truth was that they had each been assigned to bring one side dish or dessert for the holiday meals for years. The day often ended not with hugs and promises, but with angry words and hurt feelings.

The challenge with trying to emulate the Norman Rockwell painting is that it is one moment in time captured on the canvas. The painting does not show before or after the carving of the turkey. It doesn't show the piles of dishes that beg to be washed or the grocery store receipt for purchasing all the fixings.

Truth be told, I imagine every family can - and probably does - emulate that one instant of peace and harmony during the holidays, at least for an instant. It just isn't always sustainable.

We can address this third aspect by tapping on the *"hoped for happily ever"* after wishes. The key component to dig for in this aspect is the disappointment. We are not trying to negate any healthy wishes or dreams. Our objective is to be realistic and consider if our imagined future is in alignment with the truth of our past experiences.

The fourth aspect of grief is addressing all of the behaviors, attitudes and comments that "Everyone Else" exhibited around the trauma, loss or change. What, if anything, did or didn't "they" do or say?

These are often the first things to pop-up after the shock. Again, this may be due, in part, to the fact that we are often "shocked by what others do or don't do and say" at such distressing times.

This "Everyone Else" aspect often includes one form or another of your own unfinished business. When our lives come to a halt and we are forced to process a current grief, the ego mind likes to take the opportunity to heap wood on the fire by reminding us of other unresolved situations from our past when we felt disappointed, hurt or misunderstood.

I could sense I was onto something profound when I realized that these very common elements of grieving are noticeably absent in the Kübler-Ross process.

Once again, for this aspect I call on our simple movie technique and walk the client through the incident with the person or persons with which they had the conflict. I am always eager to validate the hurt, shame or disappointment that they felt; I have keen awareness of such feelings from my own story. Then, as the opportunity presents itself, we begin to explore choices. More often than not we come to some conclusions and awareness that it is highly probable that, sometime in the past, we may have inadvertently caused others similar pain with our thoughtless words or behaviors. I would hope to be forgiven for such mistakes. Please?

The final aspect of **The 5 Aspects of Grief©** was revealed and clarified for me when I was having one of those "closet days." I was fed up with feeling sad and pitiful. I wanted my life back. I no longer wanted to let my ego use grief as my excuse, my buffer or my banner. I deliberately made a decision that I would not go another day allowing my mind to tell me I was the victim of a tragedy.

First, I made a conscious and deliberate decision to "Forgive." I tapped to forgive God/ Universe, the car my son was in, the weather that was so hot that August that he was exhausted that night, the things people said or didn't say. I tapped to forgive myself for any remaining "Motherly sins of omission or commission." I tapped to forgive what people didn't do that I wish they had...on and on I tapped. I wanted to find absolutely every file that my ego had opened since my son's death.

I reviewed every story I found; I tapped, I prayed, I meditated. I was determined to release any remaining shock, regrets, imagined disappointment, hurt, fear and judgments around the experience of losing my son.

Then I made a deliberate decision to "decide to decide" how I would respond to this experience for the rest of my life. I decided that I would "Forge" ahead with open hands and heart. By working through The 5 Aspects of Grief over and over, I finally felt liberated to move into my future. It was as if I had emptied my heart and hands of all the sadness and I trained my mind to consistently focus on the joyful and loving memories of my son instead. My mantra became "No self-pity; no regrets."

You might be thinking, "It is impossible to dissolve all of the grief. It would not be realistic to think we could have no remaining hooks and triggers that around something so traumatic as the death of a child."

I wasn't sure myself until several months ago I was leading a class. As part of my usual introduction to who I am and how I got to be a tapping practitioner and trainer, I told my story. The story, of course, included the attainment of the EFT Master title and the death of my son.

At the lunch break one of the students approached me and asked "Did you really lose a child? A few of us were talking at one of the lunch tables and we were not sure if you were telling that story as a metaphor or if it was a real life experience. You just seem way too peaceful about it."

I laughed and assured her it was a real life experience. After lunch, I addressed it with the students and we were able to explore the power of tapping and the deliberate and artful use of it as a modality for healing even such traumas as losing a child.

Now, I want to mention that whenever I am working with a client, I never tell them that I am looking for The 5 Aspects of Grief while we are doing the work. I do not want their little ego mind to get distracted and focus on processes. The five aspects generally present themselves as a natural part of our sessions. If, for some reason, one or more aspects do not present naturally by the client, I am then secure in the knowledge that I do know what to look for to ensure their complete and total recovery.

Whenever I train on The 5 Aspects of Grief I always include several of The EGO Tamer® Formula's that I have developed along the way that supercharge the healing work. These formulas give us concrete tools and templates so we can methodically walk through every trauma, loss and change experience swiftly and gracefully.

I've had numerous clients who had been grieving for 10, 15, even 20 years or more, and had been unable to find peace about their trauma or loss. By intentionally seeking to explore and address The 5 Aspects of Grief and by applying the formulas, every client - without exception - experienced relief from whatever had been giving them grief - in <u>minutes</u> not months. At the conclusion of their first hour with me, they expressed that they felt lighter and more hopeful; often for the first time in years.

Occasionally, one of these clients will express remorse that they have suffered so long, needlessly. If they feel this way, I will add a few rounds of tapping to relieve the upset at the belief that they had wasted so many years stuck in grief.

Fortunately, <u>you don't need to waste another moment at the mercy of grief</u>.

I invite you to observe your jack rabbit thinking, record the stories that your mind pulls up and with a bit of tapping, heal **The 5 Aspects of Grief** once and for all!

The 5 Aspects of Grief©

G= Getting your head around it or, in some cases, Getting Over your Verdicts and Vows about it.

R= Regrets from the past (Guilt and Shame)

I= Imagined future disappointments ("Fairy Tale Endings")

E= Dealing with Everyone Else's reactions (Unfinished Business)

F= Forgive the experience and Forge Ahead

For additional instruction and free support related to **"The 5 Aspects of Grief,"** please visit our website:

www.GriefIsMourningSickness.com/5-aspects/

You can also scan the QR code below with your smartphone to visit this page.

185

Jan Luther

AFTERWORD

I hope that this book is truly helpful to you as you are finding your way through the grief in your own life after trauma, loss or change. As you gently explore the emotional and spiritual pathway through this birthing and "deathing" process, I hope you will discover the gifts and miracles that inevitably accompany such life changing experiences.

I will be thrilled if this book has introduced you to or, inspired you to use, the powerful healing tool of Tapping. Tapping is so simple that virtually anyone can learn and apply it. You can use it anywhere, at any time, and it cannot hurt you. I believe that each time you apply Tapping to a painful or traumatic experience in your life, including grief; you will be creating a deeper level of peace, health and wellness.

To find a Tapping practitioner near you, visit:

> www.AAMET.org
> www.EFTUniverse.com
> www.EFTMastersWorldwide.com
> www.EFTUnited.com

Until we meet again, I wish you peace.

Hugs,

Jan

Jan Luther